BRO
WOMEN

BROADMOOR WOMEN

TALES FROM BRITAIN'S FIRST CRIMINAL LUNATIC ASYLUM

KIM THOMAS

First published in Great Britain in 2022 by
PEN AND SWORD HISTORY
An imprint of
Pen & Sword Books Ltd
Yorkshire – Philadelphia

ISBN 978 1 52679 426 0

A CIP catalogue record for this book is available from the British Library.

Typeset in Times New Roman 12/16 by
SJmagic DESIGN SERVICES, India.
Printed and bound in the UK by CPI Group (UK) Ltd.

Pen & Sword Books Limited incorporates the imprints of Atlas, Archaeology,
Aviation, Discovery, Family History, Fiction, History, Maritime, Military, Military
Classics, Politics, Select, Transport, True Crime, Air World, Frontline Publishing,
Leo Cooper, Remember When, Seaforth Publishing, The Praetorian Press,
Wharncliffe Local History, Wharncliffe Transport, Wharncliffe True Crime and
White Owl.

For a complete list of Pen & Sword titles please contact
PEN & SWORD BOOKS LIMITED
47 Church Street, Barnsley, South Yorkshire, S70 2AS, England
E-mail: enquiries@pen-and-sword.co.uk
Website: www.pen-and-sword.co.uk

Or

PEN AND SWORD BOOKS
1950 Lawrence Rd, Havertown, PA 19083, USA
E-mail: Uspen-and-sword@casematepublishers.com
Website: www.penandswordbooks.com

Contents

Acknowledgements

This book would not have been possible without the support and help of a number of people. In particular I'd like to thank:

Dr Mark Smith, director of the MSc in English local history at the University of Oxford. It was Mark who suggested Broadmoor as a fruitful topic of research for my dissertation, which then expanded into this book.

Dr Kate Tiller, who supervised my local history dissertation and proposed taking a microhistory approach, which entailed looking in detail at individual patients and following them through their lives. Her help was invaluable.

Dr Alison Pedley, who was very generous in sharing her own research on women in Broadmoor.

Mark Stevens, county archivist at Berkshire Record Office. Mark's own book on Broadmoor was enormously helpful, but he was also kind enough to devote time to answering my numerous questions and pointing me in the direction of useful resources.

The archivists at Berkshire Record Office, and in particular Lisa Spurrier. This book was written during lockdown, which meant that, unable to visit the Broadmoor archive, I had to rely heavily on Lisa to transcribe patient files and notes, which she did ably and speedily.

My fellow local historians, in particular Rachel O'Driscoll, Karen Pagett and Lee Partridge, who all helped me with ideas and suggestions for solving historical puzzles.

Facebook friends who helped me decipher some of the illegible handwriting on nineteenth-century documents. You know who you are!

And finally: Andy and Beth, my constant companions during the year of lockdown.

Chapter 1

The Road to Broadmoor

For many of us, the word Broadmoor is enough to strike fear in the heart, immediately conjuring up a grim psychiatric institution that has housed the country's most feared criminals – people like Peter Sutcliffe, the Yorkshire Ripper; East End gangster Ronald Kray; or the Stockwell Strangler, Kenneth Erskine. These men were all initially found guilty of murder, but transferred from prison to Broadmoor when they showed signs of insanity. (Sutcliffe was later transferred back to prison.) Most of us don't know very much more about Broadmoor – when or why it was founded, or even where it is.

Yet the truth about Broadmoor is surprising, and much more interesting than its popular image would suggest. Founded in 1863, Broadmoor was the UK's first criminal lunatic asylum, designed to house people who had committed terrible crimes but were found insane at trial. A substantial and outwardly grim-looking redbrick structure set in the Berkshire countryside, Broadmoor was built only four years after nearby Wellington College, a prestigious independent school, and the two are more similar than you might expect. Both institutions consist of large, imposing buildings set in beautiful grounds: Broadmoor itself is surrounded by 130 hectares of farmland, tree-lined terraces and lawns, where the original patients could play bowls or croquet. (Today the Victorian buildings have been replaced by a bright, spacious and airy modern building that looks much like any other new hospital, apart from the high levels of security.)

Note the word 'patients'. Broadmoor was a hospital, not a prison, and its aim was not to punish wrongdoers, but to treat people who were ill. The nineteenth century saw a sea change in attitudes towards people who were considered mad, and by the time Broadmoor was built, madness – now reframed as mental illness – was very much the province of doctors. At the same time, there was a change in the legal understanding of madness, which meant that people who had committed criminal acts, including murder, could be found insane and detained indefinitely in an asylum rather than given a prison sentence.

These criminal lunatics included women as well as men. In its early days, Broadmoor had 500 patients, about 100 of whom were female. (It wasn't until 2007 that Broadmoor became a male-only hospital.) Two types of patient were admitted: those who had been found insane at trial (or unfit to plead), and convicted criminals who had been transferred after going insane in prison. In the first group, about three-quarters of the women and 40 per cent of men were in Broadmoor for murder.[1] Most of the female murderers had killed their own children – a crime much more common in the Victorian era than it is today. Those who hadn't killed their children had, for the most part, killed an adult, or committed a serious crime such as arson. The Broadmoor regime, however, was a compassionate one in which the emphasis was on curing people through a combination of nourishment, useful work and recreation. Straitjackets were rarely used, and drugs were used sparingly.

In this book, I look at the stories of seven women who spent time in Broadmoor in its early days, between 1863 and 1896, using a combination of patient files and other historical records to piece together their lives. (The files of patients admitted later are largely still closed, to protect privacy.) I will talk a little later about what a detailed look at patients' lives can teach us, but first let's take a look at the historical background that led to the establishment of Broadmoor, starting with changing attitudes towards lunacy.

From madness to mental illness

At the turn of the nineteenth century, people who were considered mad were not, for the most part, treated as a distinct category – and they were not considered to be ill. According to the historian Andrew Scull, mad people 'were assimilated into the much larger, more amorphous class of the morally disreputable, the poor, and the impotent, a group which also included vagrants, minor criminals, and the physically handicapped'.[2] Instead of being whisked away into asylums, the 'overwhelming majority of the insane were still to be found at large in the community'.[3]

There were exceptions, of course. Bethlem Hospital, or Bedlam, founded in 1330, took patients regarded as a 'danger to society'.[4] As Catharine Arnold writes, the Bedlam patients were the lucky ones: 'Others, having committed some heinous crime under the influence of their disorder, would have been summarily executed, and left to rot in a gibbet at the crossroads.'[5]

Nonetheless, not very many people ended up in Bedlam. An inspection record from 1598 shows only twenty patients in residence,[6] though by the eighteenth century this had grown to between 130 and 150.[7] Bethlem offered the very minimum in care for its inmates: an 1814 investigation found that patients were 'crammed together in a decaying structure which was acknowledged to be in need of replacement' and 'continued, for weeks and months at a time, to be chained to the walls of their cells'.[8] Beds were made of straw, food was basic (bread, cheese and beer), and much of the time they were kept in chains and manacles, and whipped for bad behaviour.

The eighteenth century saw an 'increased emphasis on providing for the indigent and disreputable in institutions'.[9] In practice, this meant that people considered mad could end up in workhouses or public gaols, along with beggars, debtors and petty criminals. There were also private asylums ('madhouses'), run for a profit, where rich people could deposit their insane or troublesome relatives. Conditions may have been better in these private asylums: a study of one such institution, Ticehurst, suggests that in the eighteenth century, 'care was taken … to foster patients' feelings of self-esteem'.[10]

At the same time, there was a growing number of charitable institutions for the 'poor but respectable classes'.[11] These included a small asylum in Norwich, founded in 1713, a ward for 'incurable lunatics' at Guy's Hospital in 1728, and other small hospitals housing about twenty or thirty patients opened in Manchester, York, Liverpool, Leicester and Exeter.

Despite the advent of these small asylums, the majority of people regarded as insane continued to be cared for – or at least tolerated – in the community. All that changed in the nineteenth century. From 1800 on, there was a large growth in public asylums run by local authorities. Many explanations have been given for this rise, but one likely explanation, put forward by Scull, is that the increased poverty associated with industrialization meant that families could no longer effectively look after members who were a drain on resources.[12] The wealthier classes, seeing the growth in poverty and the increasing numbers dependent on poor relief, saw institutions – workhouses as well as asylums – as a good way of encouraging the 'displaced peasants' who made up the bulk of the industrialized workforce to learn 'habits of thrift and industry'.[13] At the same time, Scull argues, for the first time a distinction was made between people who were simply very poor or indigent and those who were considered mad:

> The order and discipline of the whole workhouse were threatened by the presence of a madman who, even by threats and punishment, could neither be persuaded nor induced to conform to the regulations. And besides, by its very nature, the workhouse was ill-suited to provide a secure safe-keeping for those who might pose a threat to life or property.[14]

It made sense, therefore, to segregate the 'mad' into institutions where they could pose no danger or inconvenience to the rest of the community. This in turn provided an opportunity for the medical profession to extend its expertise into the realms of the disordered mind by experimenting on a (literally) captive audience. As Scull points out, there was no logical reason at that point why mad people should come under the care of doctors: the medical profession had no particular expertise to offer in terms of either diagnosis or treatment. That remained the case for a very long time, but psychiatric doctors did a good job of persuading the authorities that they were better equipped to care for the mad than lay officials. As a result, medical doctors didn't simply work in asylums – they were put in charge of running them, doing the administrative work as well as providing medical treatment.

In some of these large public asylums, inmates were often subjected to restraints such as manacles, muzzles, handcuffs and strait-waistcoats as well as physical punishment.[15] A government inquiry in 1842 into the conditions of every asylum in the country (both public and private) found some alarming practices. In one asylum, for example:

> In the small cheerless day-room of the males, with only one (unglazed) window, five men were restrained, by leg-locks … and two more were wearing, in addition, iron hand-cuffs and fetters from the wrist to the ankle; they were all tranquil. The reason assigned for this coercion was that without it they would escape … Chains were fastened to the floor in many places, and to many of the bedsteads. The males slept two to a bed …[16]

A campaign for reform led to the Lunatics Act (1845), which established a Lunacy Commission that had the power to inspect both public and private asylums. The Act also stated that every county or borough council in England and Wales should have a lunatic asylum built at public expense.[17]

One of the biggest asylums in the country was Colney Hatch, in Middlesex. Opened in 1851, it was a huge, impressive-looking building with a 'spectacular Italianate façade nearly a third of a mile long'.[18] Designed to hold 1,250 patients, it included a chapel, stable, farm and cemetery.[19] Although the idea was to provide a bright and cheerful environment for patients, the reality was somewhat different: in 1862 the inspectors described the wards as 'dark and gloomy' and found a 'deficiency of ordinary and comfortable furniture'.[20]

The introduction of county asylums was accompanied by a growth in the number of apparently mentally ill people who could be admitted to them. In 1844, asylums housed 20,893 patients, but by 1890, that number had grown to 85,352.[21] If the aim was to cure people who were mentally ill, placing them in institutions surrounded by hundreds of other mentally ill people may not have been the best way to go about it.

As asylums grew in size and number, it became clear that they housed far more than the mentally ill. They were, argues Scull, a 'dumping ground for a heterogeneous mass of physical and mental wrecks – epileptics, tertiary syphilitics, consumptives in the throes of terminal delirium, cases of organic brain damage, diabetics, victims of lead poisoning, the malnourished, the simple-minded, and those who had simply given up the struggle for existence'.[22]

By the late nineteenth century, insanity was firmly the province of the medical profession, with doctors routinely administering drugs to asylum inmates, usually purgatives and emetics or sedatives such as chloral hydrate.[23] In Showalter's words, mad people were no longer seen as 'unfeeling brutes' in need of restraint but as 'sick human beings, objects of pity whose sanity might be restored by kindly care'.[24] While on the face of it, this may seem like progress, a less rosy view – and one borne out, at least in part, by the evidence – sees medicalization as a means of exerting control over a troublesome group, with asylums isolating the mentally unwell 'both physically and symbolically from the larger society.'[25]

In this view, the 'mad' are at the mercy of a paternalistic regime that appears to have their best interests at heart yet uses psychological techniques to isolate and confine them. Paraphrasing Foucault, the most well-known proponent of this argument, MacKenzie writes that he 'saw the substitution of bonds of affection, obligation and guilt for the whips and chains of earlier methods of treatment as more insidiously cruel and repressive'.[26] More pragmatically, 'treatments' such as emetics and purgatives simply didn't work, and came to be replaced by 'moral' treatments, which were largely about providing a gentle, calming, wholesome atmosphere in which patients could recover. Of course, you don't need medical expertise to provide a calm atmosphere, and the treatment had, in fact, been pioneered, not by doctors, but by a Quaker named William Tuke, who had introduced it in the late eighteenth century in a small asylum called the York Retreat.

With their newly conferred authority, psychiatric doctors (known as 'alienists') began categorizing different types of mental illness. These attempts at categorisation were fraught with difficulty, however. As one writer pointed out:

> All who have charge of asylums must well know how very different the clear and distinct classification of books is from that medley of symptoms which is presented by real cases … to be nice in dividing instinctive insanity from moral insanity, is a subtlety more easily accomplished in books than in practice …[27]

There was a debate, which extends to the present, about the causes of mental illness. There were those who thought it had an organic cause – that something happened in the body (perhaps in the brain itself) that made people mentally ill. Others thought it might have an external cause – that particular circumstances or events could send an individual mad. There was a tendency, too, to conflate what we would now call 'learning disabilities' with mental illness. Later, Freud, who worked principally with private patients, was to develop an elaborate – and controversial – theory that saw certain physical symptoms (such as paralysis or convulsions) as arising from the repression of childhood erotic fantasies.

We now know that some of what nineteenth-century doctors labelled as mental illness was the direct manifestation of physical illness. As we have seen, people with certain types of epilepsy often ended up in asylums, as did those with syphilis, a disease that in its final stages sometimes resulted in a condition known as 'general paralysis of the insane', caused by degenerative changes in the brain. Once these diseases could either be brought under control or cured completely, these patients disappeared from the asylums.[28]

By the end of the century, there was a move away from some of the previously popular diagnostic categories to categories that are still used today, most notably dementia praecox (later renamed schizophrenia), a condition identified by the psychiatrist Emil Kraepelin. It was characterized by hallucinations and delusions, and came to be applied to mentally ill people displaying a wide range of symptoms.[29]

One of the most striking features about the diagnostic categories used by nineteenth-century doctors is the distinction between the diagnoses applied to male patients and those applied to the growing number of female patients. There has been a debate about whether doctors were increasingly likely to see madness as a female, rather than a male, condition: Elaine Showalter notes that the 1871 census shows that there were 1,182 female lunatics for every 1,000 male lunatics.[30] We can probably discount this argument, however. Joan Busfield has pointed out that women lived longer, and were therefore likely to stay in an asylum for longer periods. Analysis of admission rates shows that 'female admission rates were not routinely higher than male admission rates'.[31]

If the numbers of male and female patients who were mentally ill were roughly equal, then the types of illness with which they were diagnosed were distinctly different, with certain illnesses regarded as being more prevalent in one or other sex. Doctors, writes Showalter, saw women as 'more vulnerable to insanity than men because the instability of their reproductive systems interfered with their sexual, emotional, and rational control'.[32] The diagnosis of hysteria was taken up with enthusiasm. Referring to a particular set of physical symptoms believed to be psychological in origin, it was far more commonly applied to women than to men. As far back as the seventeenth century, hysteria was believed to be the result of the womb moving upwards through the body towards the head.[33] A woman's brain functions, the nineteenth-century doctor George Man Burrows argued, were 'intimately connected with the uterine system'.[34]

Indeed, some categories of mental illness were regarded as unique to women, who were seen as susceptible to mental illness at particular points in their reproductive life: menarche, childbirth, lactation and menopause.

This view was at least partly grounded in reality. Childbearing in the nineteenth century could be brutal and exhausting. A lack of contraception meant that a woman who married in the 1860s could expect to bear six children on average.[35] Most women gave birth without pain relief,[36] and about five in every 1,000 births resulted in the death of the mother.[37] There was a high risk of children dying: 149 out of 1,000 children died before their first birthday.[38] The principal causes were respiratory disease, diarrhoea or what was known as 'wasting disease' (premature birth and congenital defects).[39] Given that most working-class women had poor diets, and lived in cramped, crowded and unhygienic conditions, repeated childbearing would have taken a physical and mental toll. Even middle-class women did not get off lightly. Although they could at least afford the luxury of a live-in nurse to help them with a newborn, childbirth itself was not easy. In the second half of the century middle-class women started to be attended by doctors rather than midwives during birth, but it wasn't until the late 1870s that those women started to benefit from the use of chloroform for pain relief. Until then, doctors had resisted chloroform, partly on the grounds of the health risks, partly because of a religious belief that women were supposed to experience pain in childbirth.[40]

The idea that a woman might become insane after childbirth was not new (the first recorded case was that of Margery Kempe, in the fourteenth century),[41] but there was, in Hilary Marland's words, a 'massive upsurge of interest in puerperal conditions which occurred during the 1820s and 1830s, and beyond'.[42] One of the most common diagnoses was puerperal insanity, which typically occurred during the six weeks after childbirth. There were two types: melancholia and mania, of which mania, characterized by 'rumbustious behaviour' such as swearing and bellowing, was held to be more prevalent.[43] Yet there was a vagueness about whether the cause was purely physical (the result of childbirth) or related to the stresses of caring for a newborn. David Nicolson, Broadmoor's third superintendent, took a scholarly interest in the causes and treatment of insanity and argued that 'the puerperal cases of criminal lunacy' were 'often due to positive neglect or unkindness in the nursing after childbirth'.[44]

But there was no universally accepted view of what caused puerperal insanity. As Marland puts it:

> no firm conclusions could be reached, regarding its onset, preconditions, causes, prevalence, precise timing or duration, where it should be treated … how it should be treated, if it was more likely to affect first-time mothers or mothers who had borne many children, the chances of re-occurrence, and whether it would prevail most amongst undernourished, maltreated and deserted poor women or amongst well-to-do, feebly-constituted ladies for whom childbirth was considered a massive physical and mental shock.[45]

Marland argues that some cases of 'puerperal insanity' may in fact have been delusions brought on by puerperal fever, or sepsis. Appignanesi goes further, suggesting that, given the amount of time women spent childbearing, it is possible that some cases of mental illness diagnosed as puerperal mania were common-or-garden mental illnesses that simply coincided with the period after they gave birth.[46] It may be relevant that one county asylum doctor found that a quarter of puerperal insanity cases had a family history of insanity.[47]

Treatment regimes were, until the later nineteenth century, generally gentle, involving peace and quiet and nutritious food. Although regarded as a serious condition, puerperal insanity had one of the best rates of recovery of all mental illnesses: typically, women got better within a few months.[48] In an 1867 paper, Dr John Tuke relates several examples of puerperal insanity: the common feature is that after a period of bed-rest and a nutritious diet, all the women recovered.[49]

'Lactation insanity' – madness brought on by breastfeeding for too long or excessively – was another common diagnosis, though there seems to have been some blurring of the diagnostic lines between it and puerperal insanity.[50] There also seems to have been a good deal of uncertainty and fudging about the cause. It was variously attributed to women breastfeeding too little, or too much, or to women becoming fatigued and malnourished. It was held to be a particular risk for poor women, who were more likely to be undernourished and weak from anaemia.[51] But it was never entirely clear whether it was the physical act of producing milk that made women go mad, or the exhaustion that resulted from producing milk.

It's tempting to try to map nineteenth-century categories of postpartum illness onto modern categories. It's certainly the case that the melancholic form of puerperal insanity seems to be a match for what we now know as postnatal depression, while the manic form has similarities with what we now call postpartum psychosis, which is characterized by hallucinations and delusions, often of a religious nature. (Religious delusions feature heavily in contemporary accounts of puerperal insanity.) But it's hard to be conclusive, particularly as the manic form of puerperal insanity was believed to be much more common than the melancholic form, whereas today postpartum psychosis is extremely rare, affecting only one in 1,000 women. When it comes to mental health, diagnostic categories tend not to be fixed and unchanging.

The idea that insanity was expressed differently in men and women may have continued inside the asylum. In a study of Moulsford asylum, Wilcox argues that doctors judged female patients by a different set of standards from male ones: they were seen as more emotional, and traits such as 'rudeness' and swearing, or a failure to remain clean and tidy, were seen as signs of insanity in female patients.[52] This serves as a useful reminder that our ideas of madness are often cultural in nature: what might seem 'mad' in one society could seem normal in another.

Madness and criminality

The emerging view that deranged behaviour was caused by illness was reflected in changes in criminal law. When James Hadfield attempted to murder George III in 1800, he pleaded insanity, but at the time the bar for an insanity verdict was set high: a defendant had to be 'lost to all sense … that he is incapable of forming a judgement upon the consequences of the act which he is about to do'.[53] Furthermore, a defendant found insane would be set free, because there was nowhere to house him. The Criminal Lunatics Act (1800) enabled a defendant who had been found not guilty on grounds of insanity to be detained.[54]

In 1843, the McNaughton rule (spelling varies) established the test for a defence of insanity in criminal cases. Named after Daniel M'Naghten, who assassinated the prime minister's secretary, Edward Drummond, mistaking him for the prime minister himself, the rule states that to prove insanity, the defendant must be shown to have been unable, at the time of the crime, to tell right from wrong.[55]

The McNaughton rule proved controversial, even at the time. It raises very difficult questions about what constitutes criminal insanity. In some of the cases discussed in this book, the women knew what they were doing was wrong, but felt unable to stop themselves: they thought, in some cases, that God or the devil was impelling them. Nicolson pointed out the difficulties that the McNaughton rule posed for a jury: confronted with a man who was insane enough to kill his children, for example, but sane enough to know that what he was doing was illegal, the jury should have been obliged to find him guilty. In practice, Nicolson wrote, juries tended to exercise common sense and find the defendant 'not guilty on the ground of insanity'.[56]

Women, crime and criminal lunacy

Women committed fewer crimes than men,[57] though, strikingly, in the middle years of the century, they made up 40 per cent of those tried for murder.[58] (Compare this with today, where only 8 per cent of those convicted of murder are women.)[59] If we look specifically at the 1860s, half of all homicides consisted of mothers killing their own children.[60]

Infanticide (the killing of a child under the age of 1) was a crime committed almost exclusively by women, and by mid-century it was perceived as a major problem.[61] Coroners' returns for the mid-1860s show between 124 and 203 cases a year in England and Wales,[62] though this is probably an underestimate, infanticide being a relatively easy crime to conceal.[63]

The law on infanticide had changed in 1803, from a presumption of guilt on the woman's part, if she couldn't prove that the child was stillborn or had died of natural causes, to a presumption of innocence.[64] Although not treated in law as a separate category from murder, infanticide cases were generally treated with leniency.[65] The last execution for infanticide was in 1849,[66] and in cases where a newborn had died, juries usually preferred to return a verdict of 'concealment of birth'.[67] This may have been to do with the difficulty in ascertaining with any certainty that the baby had been murdered. As Lucia Zedner puts it:

> Given the difficulty of establishing whether or not the baby was born dead, died during delivery, or was deliberately killed immediately afterwards, women were often found guilty only of failing to prepare responsibly for the impending birth of their child – obviously a much lesser charge than the capital offence of child murder.[68]

There also seems to have been a good deal of sympathy towards single women who killed their newborns. The 1834 New Poor Law made illegitimate children the sole responsibility of their mothers – which 'made the prospect of raising a child almost impossible for single lower-class women'.[69] It's not surprising that poor, unmarried women killed their newborns in desperation.

Harvey Gordon, a retired Broadmoor psychiatrist, argues that the 'killing of a newborn baby or neonaticide may often have been more a form of abortion immediately after birth, rather than a product of mental illness arising after childbirth'. He adds that the killing of newborns is 'much less common where birth control, abortion and adoption are obtainable and more common in societies where illegitimate pregnancy is associated with social condemnation'.[70] Most of the women committed to Broadmoor had killed older babies and children – only 11 per cent were newborns and 38 per cent were between 1 and 5 years of age.[71] Often they killed them in a way that was impossible to disguise as death from natural causes, such as slashing their throat with a razor.

The belief that women and men were subject to different types of mental illness informed the understanding of how insanity affected criminality. This can be most clearly seen in the case of puerperal insanity, which, writes Marland, was a 'common and often successful defence strategy in infanticide and concealment trials during the mid-nineteenth century'.[72]

An increased awareness of a link between childbirth and mental illness dovetailed with the emerging view that criminal behaviour could be the result of insanity. It makes sense, therefore, that puerperal insanity and lactation insanity increasingly formed part of the defence case. The plea could, writes Marland, 'fit different infanticide scenarios, including that of the unmarried mother who quickly destroyed her new-born infant and the married woman, often exhausted by breastfeeding, who murdered an older child.'[73] There was a vagueness as to the exact point when puerperal insanity became lactation insanity. Marland argues that there were two periods of danger for women: the weeks immediately following birth, and then again a few months later 'when their health had been broken by continued efforts to breast-feed and when they themselves were in a weakened state'.[74]

Unlike certain other forms of madness, puerperal mania didn't stop those in its grip from understanding that what they were doing was wrong. On the contrary, it was characterized by 'the struggle that mothers felt … between not wanting to harm their infants and an inability to prevent themselves from doing so'.[75] This was in defiance, as we have seen, of the McNaughton rule that a plea of insanity could be accepted only where the defendant had no idea that what they were doing was wrong.[76] Furthermore, women affected by puerperal insanity could recover their sanity quickly, sometimes even by the time their case came to trial.[77]

In practice, courts tended to allow for a wider definition of insanity than that allowed by McNaughton. Uncertainty as to whether puerperal insanity had a physical or environmental cause led to an insanity plea often being tied in with a defence that the woman was poor or abused.[78] This vagueness about the causes, particularly if the bout of insanity had been short-lived, meant that the decision to accept a plea of insanity was often decided on the common-sense grounds of whether a woman had tried to cover up her crime: if she was open about what she'd done, then she was more likely to be insane.[79] Witnesses for the defence were often GPs, without psychiatric or obstetric expertise, who testified to a defendant's character as well as to her state of mind.[80]

Writing in 1902 about infanticide in the context of female criminal lunatics, John Baker, Broadmoor's deputy superintendent, says:

> The facts surrounding the commission of the deed are simple, there is rarely any attempt at concealment, except in the case of single women who endeavour to hide their shame; indeed, amongst married women, the culprit is usually the first to draw attention to the tragedy. Further, the lawyers are more than ready to accept a plea of insanity, pity inspires both judge and jury, and the opinion of the expert is not often required in evidence.[81]

One particular group – unmarried women who had killed their newborn children – were rarely found insane at trial. 'Clearly, defences of stillbirth or accident were preferable in such cases to insanity,' Ward argues.[82] As the standard sentence for concealment of birth was two years,[83] whereas a patient committed to Broadmoor could be detained indefinitely, perhaps an insanity plea was less attractive when other options were available. Furthermore, juries could be sympathetic to women who had killed their children, even when no insanity plea was made. Discussing the case of Hannah Sandles, an impoverished woman who killed her baby son in 1848, Arnot writes: 'Juries were loath to condemn women to the gallows when lamentable social conditions over which the women had little control were perceived to be important contributory factors to the crime.'[84]

One way of looking at this is to say that doctors took an essentially paternalistic view in attributing bouts of criminal insanity to a peculiarly fragile female physiology. Lucia Zedner puts it like this: 'Mental weaknesses, seen to be latent in every woman, were finally exposed by the trauma of childbirth.'[85] As the figures from Broadmoor in Table 1 show, however, it wasn't a universal diagnosis, and there was a recognition that factors such as poverty, domestic problems or intemperance could make a woman insane – as well as an admission that in many cases, the cause was unknown. (Some of the women included in the table would have killed older children rather than newborns, of course, but even in those cases the murder often followed a recent birth.)[86]

Table 1: Cause of insanity in women admitted to Broadmoor for the murder of their own children between May 1863 and April 1884

Cause of insanity	**Number**
Puerperal or lactation	52
Other reproductive	4
Melancholia	8
Congenital or hereditary	16
Poverty or domestic trouble	12
Shame, bereavement or jealousy	7
Intemperance	9
Epilepsy or other illness	6
No defined cause	35

Source: Adapted from A. Pedley, '*A painful case of a woman in a temporary fit of insanity': A study of women admitted to Broadmoor Criminal Lunatic Asylum between 1863 and 1884 for the murder of their children*, MA thesis, University of Roehampton (2012), p. 79

Furthermore, as Jade Shepherd has shown, some fathers who killed their children also successfully made pleas of insanity. There was an understanding, as with mothers, that poverty could drive a father insane enough to kill his child, and success of the plea similarly relied on evidence of previous good character: that the father had been 'kind, attentive, hardworking, and temperate'.[87]

Broadmoor: a new home for criminal lunatics

After the 1800 Act was passed, the Bethlem asylum was expanded with a new wing to house those found criminally insane; later, other asylums also took criminally insane patients. The increasing numbers of people found to be criminally insane, however, culminated in 1863 in the creation of Broadmoor.

The building was designed by Sir Joshua Jebb, an engineer who had also designed prisons in his role as surveyor-general of convict prisons – which gives us some insight into how those responsible for Broadmoor thought about it, though that differed from the perception of the people who came to run it. It was built by convict labour from local prisons.[88] The building soon met with criticism for the shoddy construction and faulty materials, and for a lack of security. Before Broadmoor opened, the first superintendent, John Meyer, insisted that the government fund particular alterations, including the replacement of brickwork and plaster, and a means, in the women's quarters, of separating the quiet patients from the violent ones. (All asylums had a policy of segregating patients according to how dangerous they were.) Stronger locks had to be fitted in the male wards. Even after all this was done, the site was found to have poor drainage, resulting in higher-than-average rates of illness in the patients in the early years.[89] The security too was far from perfect: although the site was surrounded by a perimeter fence, that didn't stop patients escaping from time to time.

Jebb's design consisted of a large central building for services and accommodation wings, supplemented by six three-storey residential blocks, consisting of a mix of dormitories and single rooms. Initially women were housed in a single block with separate wards on each of the three floors: one for particularly aggressive and high-risk patients, one for those who were low-risk, and one for those somewhere between the two.[90] When another women's block was added in 1867, the high-risk patients were put in that, while the more placid ones remained in the first block.

There was a similar division of dormitory and single-room accommodation in the male blocks. Wealthy male patients, however, could be allotted two single rooms: one for sleeping in, and one as a living room or parlour.[91] The Victorian class system was alive and well at Broadmoor. There was also a house for the medical superintendent, who lived on site. To the north side of the main building was a quadrangle containing storerooms, the kitchen, coal yard and bakery, as well as the various administrative offices. On the south side, which was reserved for patients, were planted terraces, playing fields, a kitchen garden and a farm. Between the blocks were 'airing courts', where patients could walk. Otherwise, facilities were initially basic, with little heating, inadequate lighting and poor ventilation (though central heating was introduced in 1884).[92]

The first patients to arrive at Broadmoor (nineteen women and 114 men) were all transferred from the criminal wings at Bethlem, which were then demolished. Over the next five years, another fifty-eight women and 241 men were transferred from the Fisherton House asylum in Salisbury, while thirty-two women and sixty-nine men were transferred from other asylums.[93]

By the end of 1864, there were 309 patients at Broadmoor, who between them had committed a wide range of offences. Just over a quarter (eighty-nine) had committed murder, while another fifth (sixty-one) had attempted murder.[94] Other offences, however, included burglary and housebreaking, larceny, unnatural offences, assault with intent to ravish, sheep stealing and sending threatening letters.

Once full, Broadmoor housed roughly 500 inmates at any one time, a fifth of whom were female. Between 1863 and 1900, 570 women were admitted to the asylum, of whom 242 had killed their own children.[95] About half the women were married.[96]

Approximately two-thirds of the patients were 'pleasure' patients: people who had committed a crime and either been found unfit to plead or 'not guilty by reason of insanity' and then detained 'at Her Majesty's Pleasure'. (After a change in the law in 1883, this became the slightly absurd 'guilty, but insane' – though it was eventually changed back in 1964.)[97] The rest were 'time' patients: convicts who had become insane while serving a prison sentence and then moved to Broadmoor. (In practice, many were probably insane at the time of sentencing, but not diagnosed as such until they were in prison.) Whereas the pleasure patients had often committed gruesome murders, the time patients tended to be petty but habitual criminals, guilty of offences such as larceny. Yet it was the time patients who caused Broadmoor's staff the most grief: their tendency towards criminal behaviour was undiminished, while the pleasure patients were more compliant.

What was the typical profile of the Broadmoor 'pleasure' patient? Harvey Gordon's research found that, in the 1860s, the mean age of male 'pleasure' patients was 42, while for women it was 38. Amongst the men, 39 per cent had committed homicide, and 33 per cent another violent offence. More than three-quarters of the men (77 per cent) remained at Broadmoor until they died.

Of the women, 74 per cent of pleasure patients had committed homicide, and 19 per cent another kind of violent crime. In the vast majority of cases, the victim was their own child. (Even in the 1950s, two-thirds of female pleasure patients admitted to Broadmoor had killed their own child; in the 1960s, when contraception became freely available, the proportion dropped dramatically to one in four.) Of the female pleasure patients admitted in the 1860s, nearly two-thirds remained until they died, and of the remaining 35 per cent, 'those who were conditionally discharged stayed an average of five and a half years, and those transferred to local asylums stayed an average of 22 years'.[98]

The class background of men and women was markedly different too. Almost all the women admitted had a working-class job, such as domestic servant, or were married to a man who had a manual or labouring job. But only half the men admitted had labouring or manual jobs, and the first annual report, published in 1865, lists a wide range of occupations for the male patients, including pianoforte maker, publican, toll maker, hairdresser and castrator. Similarly, most of the men could read and write, while only a third of women could do so.[99] Indeed some of the male patients, such as the artist Richard Dadd and the surgeon George Houlton, came from highly privileged backgrounds.

The cost of looking after the patients was met partly by central government, with additional funds coming from the local authorities where the patients resided, or, in some cases, the trustees of property belonging to the patients. For each patient, the cost of care amounted to approximately £47 per year, roughly the equivalent of £4,000 today.[100]

When patients were admitted, the staff made an attempt at diagnosis. The diagnostic categories used were ones we would barely recognize today: insanity was either the result of 'moral circumstances' (such as intemperance, vice and religious excitement) or physical conditions, such as head injuries, fever and childbirth. The first annual report includes causes such as jealousy, disease of brain, religious excitement and masturbation. Yet in the majority of cases, the doctors didn't come up with any diagnosis at all: the cause of their insanity was listed as 'unknown'.[101]

Life in Broadmoor

The intention was that Broadmoor would provide a soothing environment, not a punitive one. One patient wrote home that

Broadmoor was 'pleasantly situated, has an extensive view and is very healthy … we have good food … clean clothes, good beds and bedding. … [we] are treated with kindness by the officials placed over us, and have free conversation among the other patients'.[102]

In contrast to other asylums of the time,[103] patients were not given drugs other than stimulants or sedatives.[104] Measures such as 'binding the breasts and drug therapies aimed at modifying production of menses and breast milk' were used with women who had recently been pregnant and had killed their own children, however.[105]

The underpinning philosophy was of 'moral treatment', which consisted of exercise and occupation, 'regular meals' and 'plenty of fresh air'.[106] The day began with prayers, at 6 am in the summer, 7 am in winter, and thereafter was mostly filled with paid work, at least for those patients capable of it (about half). Those without skills undertook 'the endless washing, scrubbing and polishing required to keep the asylum spotless'.[107] The more skilled were able to undertake jobs such as making and repairing clothing, bookbinding, or gardening,[108] growing produce such as potatoes, turnips, peas and gooseberries. Jobs were strictly sex segregated, with women undertaking laundry and needlework duties,[109] making or mending items for use inside the asylum, such as petticoats, tablecloths, shirts and towels. (All the clothes worn by patients, including boots and shoes, were made on the premises.)[110] Mealtimes were bland affairs: a typical evening meal would include meat, potatoes, carrots and parsnips, with weak beer to drink and fruit pies or suet pudding for dessert. The women were given smaller portions than the men.[111] In the evening, there would be prayers again. There was also, however, leisure time, during which patients could make use of a library and a day room.

It was clearly an austere life involving hard work, unexciting food and a daily dose of religion. Being separated from family and friends for an indefinite period of time must have felt unbearably lonely for some. It's not surprising that sometimes patients tried to escape.

Yet for poorer patients, Broadmoor may well have afforded a welcome change from their previous life. Of Broadmoor's first inmate, Mary Ann Parr, Mark Stevens writes that her 'quality of life inside the walls was probably significantly better than she had enjoyed outside. She had a roof over her heard, and she did not have to worry about food or money'.[112] He adds: 'This was the asylum as refuge: by removing a patient from their day-to-day life, the Victorians believed they would be able to neutralize whatever factor was causing their insanity, leading to beneficial results.'[113]

One of the more agreeable aspects of Broadmoor life was the opportunity for friendships to develop. In the dayroom, women could sit and chat, read books or magazines, and take part in games such as chess, draughts, dominoes, backgammon and cribbage. There was even a piano provided for their use.[114] The women also worked alongside each other while doing the laundry or needlework. One woman wrote to the superintendent after she had been released from Broadmoor:

> I am conscious to know if L.T. is still under your care, if so, will you give me some hope of her liberty. I have long neglected her, but now I have a home of my own and most freely will I share it with her, it is my husband's wish that I should send to you about it, for he is most anxious that we should do our best for her, if such a thing were possible, she would have every opportunity of getting on, as I am well known in the town, and have plenty of work, Dear Sir, I can hardly expect you to give me an answer to my letter as I have been so negligent … I beg of you to give me some hopes for L.T., if she is still under your care, will you kindly remember me to all of them, and also to the officials. I am glad to tell you that I have excellent health, I trust that your lady and family are quite well.[115]

Many of the patients retained some form of contact with the outside world. As Jade Shepherd points out, working-class families did not 'typically exchange (or keep) regular letters' so these are a 'highly valuable' source providing insight into the impact on family life of having a member in the asylum.[116] Shepherd, who has analysed the letters family members sent to their relatives in Broadmoor, argues that they demonstrate the closeness of family relationships:

> family ties and affective relationships mattered a great deal to working-class Victorians. Some found new ways to give meaning to their relationship with their incarcerated relative despite the distance between them, and they sought to give meaning – via their words and actions – to their relative's life despite the hardships their committal into Broadmoor had caused.[117]

Many husbands, she notes, wrote letters to the superintendent petitioning for their wives' release – in some cases, this may have been simply because they were unable to cope with bringing up young children alone, but in others, they seemed to be genuinely supportive. A number of mothers, too, wrote to their daughters to let them know how their families were faring. Some wrote to the superintendent asking for their release. One wrote: 'take pity on her poor aged mother that has been deprived of my dear daughter so many years I cannot express my heartfelt grief … relieve me of this distress and restore my daughter to me again.'[118]

Many of the stories shared in this book bear out Shepherd's statement that the Broadmoor archive 'is a repository of love, sorrow, and hope, alive with stories of loss, poverty, desperation and kinship'.[119]

Like any institution housing multiple occupants, Broadmoor was affected every time there was an epidemic: in the 1890s, there were several waves of flu, for example, and in 1890, the disease affected ninety-four patients, of whom three died. Yet, relatively speaking, Broadmoor took good care of its patients: between 1863 and 1881, the mortality rate of criminal lunatics in other asylums was 5.7 per cent, while in Broadmoor it was less than half that, at 2.5 per cent.

After the first superintendent, John Meyer, died in May 1870, his replacement, William Orange, introduced a humane regime in which 'arts, crafts and sports flourished'.[120] Visits from family and friends were encouraged. Orange even laid on entertainments for the patients: male patients took part in concerts while female patients held a fortnightly dance. A brass band was formed of staff and patients and performed at the various events. Orange was succeeded in 1886 by David Nicolson, who stayed in post until 1896, and continued his predecessor's approach. A choral society was formed to sing light operetta, and staff and patients put on a performance of *HMS Pinafore*, in which Nicolson himself performed.[121] The regime at Broadmoor was undoubtedly paternalistic, but compared with the harshness of many ordinary asylums,[122] it offered a relatively benign environment.

The later nineteenth century saw a rise in 'psychiatric pessimism' – a belief amongst doctors that insanity was hereditary and that a cure could not be found. As a result, some asylums saw the reintroduction of restraints and seclusion.[123] In contrast, Meyer, Orange and Nicolson maintained a firm belief in treating patients with kindness, and in 1888 Nicolson wrote that he had no intention of copying other asylums by reintroducing restraints.[124] When Nicolson retired in 1896, however, he was succeeded by Richard Brayne, who had previously been the medical governor of a prison. Sadly, Brayne's regime was less humane, and he has been described as 'widely feared and loathed'.[125]

Leaving Broadmoor

Although Broadmoor patients were detained indefinitely, the length of stay varied a good deal. The decision to discharge patients was made by the home secretary, and a study by Jonathan Andrews of both Broadmoor and Perth Criminal Lunatic Asylum between 1860 and 1920 showed that well over half of the child-murderers were discharged as recovered, with 'female offenders being especially likely to obtain their release'.[126] In a sample of ninety-two female Broadmoor infanticide cases, Andrews found that sixty-three were conditionally released, while two died, seven were removed to other asylums and one killed herself.[127] Of those conditionally discharged, the average length of stay was just over eight years.[128]

The question of whether a woman could become pregnant again, and therefore come under the influence of puerperal insanity, was one factor in deciding whether to discharge a patient: once past the menopause, women who had experienced puerperal insanity were generally considered safe – though menopause itself was regarded as a time when women could become insane.[129]

This concern was not, however, the decisive factor. Other important considerations included whether there were relatives who were willing to look after the discharged patient and whether those relatives were respectable. A 'significant proportion' of women in Broadmoor had come from abusive domestic situations, which made them less likely to be discharged. Sometimes the local constabulary were enlisted to monitor women who had been released.[130]

Nineteenth-century Broadmoor, then, was not as fearsome a place as we might imagine. It can hardly have been described as a happy institution, given that most of the patients were deeply troubled individuals who had committed terrible crimes and then been forcibly separated from their own families. By today's standards, it might have seemed cheerless: a cold and draughty environment, a diet of bland food and a day filled with largely menial work. Yet for some it would have been a welcome retreat from lives of unremitting toil, and the prevailing ethos was kind, rather than punitive: Orange and Nicolson did their best to make Broadmoor a gentle environment in which severely mentally ill patients were given the best possible help to recover.

Seven women

In the following chapters, I will share the stories of individual women who spent time at Broadmoor in the late nineteenth century. These stories are interesting for two reasons.

One is that they offer a unique insight into Victorian attitudes to, and treatment of, women who were criminally insane. The other is that Broadmoor's substantial archive, which first became available to the public in 2008, gives a glimpse into the lives of people who would otherwise have left very little trace in the historical record. Ordinary working-class women such as those who feature in this book rarely wrote about their experiences, so we know very little about their lives: what we do know comes from the times when they came into contact with officialdom, such as the legal system. Documents available from the Broadmoor archive include patient case files, admissions books, discharge records and reports by the medical superintendent and inspectors, giving us a glimpse into these women's stories.

Combine the patient files with newspaper reports and trial transcripts, and it's possible to learn a lot about these women's lives. Sometimes we even hear their own voices, though for the most part their experiences are mediated through the writings of doctors and officials. By combining the different sources, we can start to reconstruct their lives and something of the social context in which they lived – an approach known by historians as 'microhistories'. The idea of a microhistory is that a close look at the life of a single person can provide us with a broader knowledge of marriage, family and kinship ties, local communities, the stresses of working life and poverty, and the importance of religion. Or, as the historian Christopher French puts it: 'microhistory can provide much valuable information on the "macro-questions" of life, work and death.'[131] I take some of my inspiration from Halle Rubenhold's excellent book *The Five*, which uses a similar approach to construct a narrative of the lives of the Jack the Ripper victims.[132]

The seven women had a variety of backgrounds and life experiences: Mary France, for example, was an illiterate miner's wife from Lancashire, who struggled to make ends meet, while Julia Spickernell lived a relatively comfortable life in London with her husband, one of a new breed of white-collar workers. Another young woman, Blanche Bastable, was brought up on a Dorset farm. Six of the women were married, and five were mothers, giving birth multiple times. Four were sent to Broadmoor for killing their own children, while one killed her husband, another killed her mother and one attempted to kill the woman taking care of her.

Four of the seven women had experienced recent bereavements of siblings or children shortly before committing their crimes, and one wonders if the trauma of the loss played a part in their mental illness, though it's not something that either the doctors or the lawyers seem to have considered. Another was the victim of prolonged domestic abuse, and here they did make the connection, believing that her husband's cruelty had driven her to a temporary madness.

Despite their similarities, each woman's story is unique, and each one will, I hope, shed light on what it was like to be a woman in the Victorian era, the importance of family ties and the prevailing attitudes towards criminality and madness.

Chapter 2

Mary France

Mary Bramwell was born on 8 March 1847 in Aspull, in the borough of Wigan in Lancashire, and baptized six days later at St David's, the local Haigh parish church. Although her parents Thomas and Jane were aged only 24 and 22 respectively, they had already been married four years, and Mary's elder brother John had been born in 1844. All nine of the Bramwells' children were baptized in the Anglican church – as were Mary's own children.

Aspull had once been a tiny village inhabited by tenant farmers – there are references to it as far back as the thirteenth century. But like many northern towns and villages, it underwent dramatic change during the industrial revolution. The Wigan Coal and Iron Company, the biggest colliery owner in the Lancashire coalfield, operated four coalmines in Aspull, employing 1,000 workers. At the same time, the cotton industry was in full swing, and Aspull saw its population increase from 2,772 in 1848[1] to more than 8,952 in 1891.[2] The Bramwells were typical inhabitants: Thomas was a coal miner, and Jane had been a cotton weaver before marriage.

Mary was born into grinding poverty. Life was particularly hard for mining families, and Lancashire colliers worked twelve-hour days[3] for low pay – typically about 20 shillings (£1) or 25 shillings a week.[4] A fixed wage wasn't guaranteed, but was dependent on how much coal was mined: a miner whose tub was not perfectly full would receive no pay.[5] Men were charged for tools, and fines imposed for 'unsatisfactory' work. A miner 'could never know what he would be earning the following week, let alone the following year'.[6] As a job, it was both dangerous and physically arduous, and miners were susceptible to a variety of industrial diseases.[7] 'It is universally recognized,' Engels wrote, 'that such workers enter upon old age at forty.'[8]

Living conditions for the Bramwells would have been cramped. Typically, families rented accommodation from private landlords; public housing was a later development. Overcrowding in Wigan was rife and, at the middle of the nineteenth century, it was regarded as 'one of the unhealthiest towns in the country'.[9] The 'small, dark, damp, insanitary buildings' in which many coalmining families lived, combined with 'the polluted water supplies and inefficient waste and refuse disposal' meant that disease was rampant.[10] It wasn't just the houses that were dark and unhygienic: Engels wrote of Bolton (one of the nearest big towns to Aspull) that 'the older part of the town is especially ruinous and miserable' and that 'a dark-coloured body of water, which leaves the beholder in doubt whether it is a brook or a long string of stagnant puddles, flows through the town and contributes its share of the total pollution of the air, by no means pure without it.'[11] Jane and Thomas were lucky enough to see most of their children survive infancy, though two sons died before reaching their first birthday. Figures for Sheffield show that half the city's children died before the age of 5.[12]

Life in Lancashire's mining villages could be brutal: as Raymond Challinor, in his book on the Lancashire and Cheshire miners, writes: 'Miners' social life was inevitably affected by living amid squalor, dirt and degradation.'[13] Their pastimes generally involved drinking, gambling and violent games such as 'purring,' which Challinor describes as 'a game of football played without the unnecessary complication of using a ball. Two men just kicked each other's shins until one stumbled and was then battered into insensibility.'[14] The fun came from betting on the result. It was also, says Challinor, a way of settling a score with an adversary, and, unfortunately, a 'means of showing displeasure with one's wife and children'. One of the reasons for the viciousness of the injuries was that, according to a local coroner of the time, Lancashire people tended to wear clogs with 'wooden soles with narrow toes bound with iron and tin'. He added that 'they form most dangerous weapons, and are readily resorted to on the smallest provocation'.[15] In the space of a single week in August 1874, Challinor records five incidents of people being kicked to death in Lancashire, three of them women.[16]

This background brutality forms only part of the picture, however. Religion was still a dominant force in the region; although on the day of the 1851 census, less than 30 per cent of Wigan's population attended a church service,[17] the real proportion of working-class people attending church was probably much higher. As McLeod has pointed out, the census 'counted attendance on a single day, and so missed some of those who attended regularly, but not every Sunday'.[18]

By the middle of the century, nonconformity was on the rise in Britain, with Methodist and Baptist churches springing up in many working-class areas, particularly South Wales. Its influence was unevenly distributed, however, and the Established Church maintained a strong hold amongst the working classes of west Lancashire.[19] One possible reason for this is that the area had a substantial Catholic presence, so people clung more rigidly to their Protestant identity (or as one commentator puts it: 'Protestant consciousness was more fully developed than elsewhere.')[20]

Just as nonconformity was closely associated with support for the Liberal Party, Anglicanism and Conservatism tended to go hand in hand: 'In Lancashire more than any other part of the country both working-class Toryism and working-class Anglicanism were major forces, and very often the two causes were supported by the same people.'[21]

The Bramwell family's allegiances were to the Anglican tradition, and it is likely that this lent weight to the characterization of Mary's family as 'respectable' when she was later charged with murder.

McLeod notes that 'respectability' was a 'key concept in Victorian England, with great resonance for many working-class people', that

> it was a crucial part of the working-class understanding of the term that manual work was as honourable as any other, and that a working-class family who worked hard, lived 'decently', were independent and brought up their children to be good citizens, were entitled to the same respect as the member of any other class who did these things.[22]

The Bramwells, then, were almost certainly the type of family who lived decently, rather than the type of family whose members were engaged in heavy drinking sessions or kicking other people to death.

After Mary was born, Thomas and Jane had seven more children: James, Ellen, Thomas, Nancy, Jane, Alice and Henry. James, born in 1849, lived for only a few months, as did Thomas, born in 1853. The youngest, Henry, was born in 1863. Mary probably didn't go to school – there is no record of her doing so, and in later life, she was illiterate, marking her name with a cross rather than a signature. The children went out to work young. By 1861, the eldest child, John, still living at home, was working as a coalminer, while 14-year-old Mary, like many of her contemporaries, was a reeler in a factory – a job in the cotton mill that involved operating the machine that wound the yarn onto the bobbin.[23]

This job formed one small part of a complicated chain of processes that the cotton would go through. Each part of the chain took place in a different room, and employed different people to carry it out. The process began with raw cotton fed into machines to open, clean and blend the fibres: after that, the stages included using machines to remove tangles, putting the cotton through a series of frames to create a manageable yarn known as a 'roving', spinning to pull the roving thinner, and then winding on to a cone by a worker who would remove the lumps and irregularities. Half those cones became the weft thread that would go across the loom and half became the warp thread that would run down the length of the material. The weft threads were wound onto small bobbins, or weft pirns, to go into the shuttle for the weaver. The women who did this job were known as 'reelers' or 'creelers' – this was the work that Mary was employed in. Like all the cotton mill jobs, reeling was repetitive and tedious.

In the final stage of the process, the warp threads went to the beamer, a man who drew the ends of the cotton onto a long, cylindrical beam, which then passed through a solution known as sizing onto a second beam. From the winding rooms, the cotton was taken to the weaving sheds, where each weaver would be in charge of two to four looms. This is where the bulk of mill workers were employed.[24]

The jobs in the mill were at least partly segregated by sex, and there was a big disparity in wages. The mule spinners, for example, were all male, and in the late nineteenth century paid about 41 shillings a week (just over £2). Both men and women worked as weavers, the women earning approximately 21 shillings and the men 25 shillings. The mills also employed children in some unskilled roles, who were paid even less – girls earned only an average of only five shillings a week.[25]

Work in the cotton mill was dangerous and accident-prone, and cotton mill hands were susceptible to industrial diseases caused by fibre dust.[26] On the other hand, for those like Mary who worked in the winding room, the one benefit was that it was quieter than work in the weaving room: the women could talk to each other without resorting to lip reading, which was how those working in the weaving rooms, filled with the din of hundreds of looms, communicated.

Mill work was also regarded as a more respectable job for women and girls than the alternative, which was to work above ground – the 'pit brow' – at the mine.[27] Women who worked at the pit brow were generally thought of as being less feminine and having loose morals.[28]

In October 1868, Mary, aged 21, gave birth to an illegitimate son, James. The baby was baptized on 27 December 1868, but neither his birth certificate nor the baptism record name a father, and in the space where the father's occupation is normally listed, Mary is described as a 'spinster'. By the time James was born, illegitimacy rates had fallen to about four births in 100, and it was common for an illegitimate birth to be followed by a marriage.[29] Mary, then, was particularly unlucky.

We have no way of knowing who James's father was, and it's not impossible, of course, that Mary was raped. Whatever happened, she retained the support of her parents, and it seems that James was cared for by Mary's mother while she worked – a common arrangement that supports Angela John's statement that mining families were 'particularly close-knit' and that the concept of familial support 'went beyond a reciprocation of duties and services or occasional help in times of crisis'.[30] Indeed, the support of close family ran like a thread through Mary's life, during the darkest times and right up until her death.

John, meanwhile, had left home to get married and in 1869 his wife gave birth to a baby daughter. In 1871, Mary, 24, her son James, and her younger siblings still lived at home in Gullet, Aspull. All four of the older girls, including 13-year-old Jane, worked as cotton mill hands, while the two youngest children were still at school.

Having five members of the house in employment, even if the four cotton mill hands earned only a pittance, may have eased the financial burden for Thomas and Jane of having a large family to bring up. For many households, the adult male wage was not enough to support a family, and the historian Barry Reay has argued that many working-class families relied on a collective endeavour known as the 'social economy', of which 'the work of children was a linch-pin'.[31]

There was one more occupant in the house in 1871: a lodger named George France, aged 20 and also a collier.

Houses in mining villages were typically so small that families had to share one or two rooms.[32] With the addition of George, conditions must have been exceptionally cramped. But taking in a lodger was a common way of making ends meet: in 1851, one in seven of the households of non-agricultural labourers had a lodger, usually a single man.[33]

On 27 March 1871, Mary and George married at St George's Church. While George's occupation is recorded as collier, Mary's is left blank, so she must have given up her work at the cotton mill on her marriage, in line with convention among miners' wives.[34] The certificate shows them both as living in Whelley, one of the main streets in Aspull, rather than in Gullet, where they had lived with Mary's parents. George and Mary were to move several times during the course of married life, probably because of the precariousness of maintaining a tenancy on a low and unpredictable wage. Privately rented housing was much more expensive than colliery housing, and profiteering amongst landlords was rife.[35]

George was four years younger than Mary. He had been born in Dukinfield, Cheshire, to John and Elizabeth France. Although the marriage certificate records his father's job as collier, John had previously worked as a greengrocer. (In the 1851 census he is described, less grandly, as a potato dealer.) By 1861, when George was 10, John had died, and Elizabeth had taken work as a charwoman to make ends meet. George had two older sisters: Ellen, 15, who was working as a cotton weaver, and Sarah, 12 who worked as a silk piecer (a job in the silk industry that involved joining broken silk threads together). He also had a brother two years younger, Joseph. Their family, too, had a lodger, 27-year-old Moses Silcox, who was also a coal miner.

Although Mary had given up paid work, life as a miner's wife was a hard slog. Home comforts were minimal: without a bathroom, the family would have shared an outside lavatory with other households. A fire in the back room would have been the only source of warmth, and Mary's day would have started by getting up in the cold, laying a new fire and cleaning out the grate. The fire was also the only means of heating water for a cup of tea or for bathing or laundry. Pithead baths didn't exist until well into the twentieth century, so George would have come home filthy and washed in a tin bath in front of the fireplace. Once a week, Mary would have had to heat up enough water to wash the family's clothes. This was a back-breaking manual task, involving putting the clothes in a tub of hot water and then moving them around with a dolly (a wooden pole with six legs at the bottom). She may have used a mangle to wring the water out of the clean clothes, which would then probably have been dried on a clothes horse in front of the fire.

Dirt would have been a constant problem, as soot from the fire had a tendency to get everywhere, covering clothes and furniture with grime. Sweeping, dusting and scrubbing floors were unavoidable daily chores. Once babies started to arrive, they added an additional burden of feeding and clothing, as well as requiring homemade cloth nappies that had to be rinsed, washed and dried frequently.

And arrive they soon did. The couple already had Mary's illegitimate son, James, living with them, though he didn't take George's name. Their first child together, Ellen, was born in April 1872, and baptized at a licensed Church of England chapel at a large private estate known as Hindley Hall. The joy of a newborn was short-lived, however: in October 1873, Ellen died of convulsions. By this stage, the family had undertaken the first of their many moves, to a street called Birchall's Row.

George and Mary lost two more children from respiratory diseases – one of the most common causes of infant death in the nineteenth century.[36] Thomas, born in 1874, died of bronchitis, aged 8 months, in April 1875. His death was registered by Mary; unable to write, she marked her name with an X. Jane, born in 1878, died in January 1880, also of bronchitis, only 15 months old. The middle child, Joseph, born in 1876, survived into adulthood, as did Betsy, born in 1881, and Jane, born in 1883.

There was a further blow for Mary when her father, Thomas, died in 1880, at the age of 57, of chronic rheumatism and liver disease. (According to Mary's Broadmoor record, there was no intemperance in the family, so the liver disease was not related to drinking.) Jane remained in Aspull, and in 1881 still had her three adult daughters (Nancy, Jane and Alice, all working in the mill, as Mary had done, as cotton reelers) at home, along with 17-year-old Henry, now a miner. Jane, living at 1, Lower Gullet, was not too far from her daughter and son-in-law, now living at 96, Lower Gullet. Amongst the tragedy, there was one cause for cheer: in 1875, 7-year-old James, Mary's illegitimate son, began attending Aspull Church of England Primary School.

For a family who just managed to scrape by, it must have been a bitter blow when George, who was employed by the Wigan Coal and Iron Company, one of the giants of the coalmining regions,[37] fell victim to the system of fines imposed by the company on their workers – a system that was backed by the force of law. At the County Sessions, George was fined 5s, with costs, for 'disobeying the rules at the Gorse's Pit'. He had asked for the cage to be lowered so he could be sent to the top without the authority of the hooker-on.[38]

In 1886, the four surviving children (James, Joseph, Betsy and Jane) welcomed a new sibling, Ellen. (It was common for families to give a new baby the same name as a child that had died.) On 22 August, Ellen was baptized at Aspull's new church, St Elizabeth's, which had been built only four years earlier.

By now, Mary must have been physically and mentally exhausted. Not only was the life of a miner's wife 'one long round of chores and drudgery',[39] but in the space of ten years, she had given birth to six children, three of whom had died. Perhaps giving birth again at the age of 39 tipped her over the edge: George told staff at Broadmoor that after Ellen's birth, she became 'altered in manner and sleepless'.

There may have been other causes too. At some point, we know from Mary's record that she had jumped out of a factory window, two storeys high, and injured her head. Why or when she did this we don't know. But after that, she was dazed for some time and suffered from headaches. One of her cousins was in an asylum, so there may have been a hereditary element, and, according to her Broadmoor case notes, three of her own children suffered from fits.

Even more significant is the fact that, according to her Broadmoor notes, she suffered from 'exophthalmic goitre', another term for Graves' disease. An autoimmune condition, Graves is far more common in women than men, and is often triggered by pregnancy. It frequently causes hyperthyroidism, which results in, among other things, muscle weakness, sleeping problems, fast heartbeat and bulging eyes. Graves can also cause cognitive impairment and psychosis, including delusions and hallucinations.[40] In other words, it seems more than likely that Mary's mental health problems were the result of a physical illness triggered by the birth of her last child.

At any rate, by December, there were signs that Mary's mental state was unstable. The children had been ill, she was unable to sleep and her tongue began to swell (another symptom of Graves' disease). On Thursday, 16 December, she began talking about religion, telling George that she had committed so much sin that she would not be forgiven.

George was worried enough about Mary's mental state that, on Saturday morning, 18 December, he asked her mother to look after her. Mary got up early with George to prepare his breakfast. She asked him not to go to the pit, but he had been doing so badly recently – a poignant illustration of the harsh impact of the piece rate payment system – that he told her he had to go.[41] Mary mentioned that she had been dreaming about her father, who she believed to be in heaven. It was a place, she thought, where she would never go, as she had 'rebelled against God and sinned'. She believed that she could see Jesus, but that Satan 'was holding her back from touching him'. George tried to pacify her by telling her that it was her imagination, and to take the medicine the doctor had prescribed. On the way to work, he called in to see his mother-in-law and told her the time Mary needed to take her medicine.

Jane Bramwell went over to her daughter's house and saw her dress her children, and they then walked over to Jane's house to have some tea. Mary, Jane was later to tell the inquest, had seemed 'middling quiet' and had returned home to 'brush about a bit'.

When Mary arrived home from her mother's house, she picked up a paring knife, walked over to baby Ellen's bed and slashed her throat. Having done this, she walked across the fields to Westhoughton where she caught a train to Bolton. Finding a policeman on duty near the town hall, she gave herself up, still with blood on her hands. While detained, she 'talked freely about the act' but 'interluded her statements with rambling references to the Holy Ghost and kindred subjects'. The police seem to have understood immediately that Mary was mentally unwell. A newspaper report stated that they 'have treated her with every consideration' and incarcerated her in a day room rather than a cell. In the meantime, one of the children had come to fetch Jane, who went to Mary's house and found Ellen in bed with her throat cut.

On Saturday night, George was allowed to talk to his wife. According to the newspaper report, he 'appeared heartbroken by the catastrophe which has blighted his home'. On Sunday, Mary was visited by 'several relatives'. Another newspaper account of the killing concludes with the words: 'The family is very respectable, and much commiseration is expressed the neighbourhood.'[42] It's just a few words, but it suggests a close-knit community where the Frances were known and liked. Later, George was to tell an inquest that 'No better mother could be found in Aspull than his wife had been to his children'.[43] The family doctor, Dr McLaughlin, also gave evidence to the inquest, saying that he had visited Mary a few weeks earlier when her children were ill and that she had been 'suffering from want of rest and worry'. He also said of her that 'she seemed an exceptionally good Mother, excessively fond of her children and nursed them very well'.[44] The event seems to have been perceived by everyone involved as a tragedy rather than as a crime.

It seems that the stress of the family's series of personal tragedies had been exacerbated by the children's illnesses, Mary's lack of sleep and a shortage of money – and of course, by the Graves' disease. But what emerges from the inquest testimony most clearly is the strength of the family relationships: Mary's grief for her late father, George's concern for his wife and efforts to help her and Jane's attempts to soothe her daughter by having her around for tea. Many historians in the past thought that industrialization had weakened the ties in working-class families, yet it seems more likely that it strengthened them. As one historian, Trevor Griffiths, wrote, industrialization succeeded in 'consolidating relationships within the nuclear household … Family unity thus rested on a sense of mutual dependence, enforced by recurrent crises.'[45]

In the initial court hearing, held at the County Petty Sessions in Bolton on 20 December, Mary was described as being 'of very respectable appearance' and also 'of delicate appearance'. Sergeant Lomax, the police officer called to the Frances' house, gave evidence that the knife used to commit the crime was found near the body: 'It was an ordinary shoemaker's knife, like the knives commonly used for peeling potatoes.'[46]

At the inquest, held on 21 December, the coroner recommended a verdict of 'wilful murder', which the jury duly returned.[47]

After her arrest, Mary was detained in Manchester's newly opened Strangeways prison. On 29 January 1887, the *Wigan Observer and District Advertiser* published a report of the trial, which took place at Manchester Assizes.[48] It seems to have been over relatively quickly. Mary was charged with killing her infant daughter by 'cutting its throat with a shoemaker's knife'. The report describes her as having 'a most vacant look upon her face' and that she 'paid no attention to anything taking place around her'. Mary took no notice of the request to enter a plea, and two expert witnesses – Dr Ley, superintendent of the

Prestwich Lunatic Asylum, and Dr Paton, the Strangeways surgeon – gave evidence as to Mary's state of mind, with Ley describing her as 'incapable of understanding the incidents of a trial' and her mind as a 'perfect blank'. In Paton's view, her mind was a 'complete wreck'. There seems to have been no attempt to attribute Mary's state of mind to puerperal or lactation insanity. Under the judge's direction, the jury found the prisoner unfit to plead. The judge ordered that Mary be detained 'during her Majesty's pleasure'.[49]

When Mary arrived at Broadmoor, David Nicolson had been in post for a year, and his annual report reveals that there were 531 inmates: 392 men and 139 women.[50] In the course of the year, twenty-nine men and fourteen women were admitted. Of those fourteen, ten were admitted for murder, in all cases of their own children.[51]

During her time at Broadmoor, Mary made a gradual recovery. At the beginning, she was still clearly mentally ill. Noting her religion as 'Protestant', her admission record states that she is 'under a delusion that "she is the Lord Jesus Christ" and that "she is in heaven" but sometimes says she's in hell – also that her soul is lost'. Her bodily health is described as 'fair' and next to the question as to whether she is suicidal or dangerous, the record says she is 'occasionally dangerous'. It also says that her 'memory' is 'gone'. The cause of her insanity is recorded as 'not known'. Notes from her first year describe her as a 'dark low spirited depressed looking little woman … is very melancholic, thinks her soul is lost and that she is going to be taken away from here to be killed. Says "You won't let them take me away", "You won't send me away"'.

In April she is described as 'still very low spirited and miserable, afraid that something is going to happen' but by September her notes say that she is 'still low spirited at times but has been more cheerful of late'. By January 1888 she was 'slowly improving from the melancholic condition she was in on admission'. A year later her notes state: 'Mentally is brighter and more cheerful. Very deaf.' (The deafness is likely to have been caused by the Graves' disease.)

No doubt being separated from her family and placed among strangers would have been a profoundly lonely and disorienting experience for Mary. We don't know if George or any other family member was able to visit: the cost in time and money of a nine-hour train journey from Wigan to Crowthorne would have been prohibitive for a Lancashire coalminer.

But there would have been some material advantages for Mary too, and she was probably well looked after at Broadmoor. Nicolson was no doubt proud of the fact, stated in his annual report, that there were no casualties 'of a serious kind' during the year and 'it was not found necessary to have recourse to mechanical restraint in any form whatever'.[52] There were no outbreaks of epidemic disease and the inspectors' report noted the 'cleanliness of the wards, and indeed of all parts of the asylum'.[53] To celebrate Queen Victoria's Golden Jubilee in June 1887, inmates were given a dinner of roast beef and plum pudding.[54]

Mary would have benefitted from regular meals, and freedom from the hard, daily grind of childcare and housework, though as she began to recover, she would have been expected to engage in laundry and cleaning duties. Away from the grime of the coal mines and cotton mills, she might have enjoyed the fresh air, gardens and tranquillity of Broadmoor. Many of the wards had recently been repainted and decorated, and the female block was now heated by hot water.[55]

Within only a few months, however, George was asking for her to be released, a request he was to make six times in all. The historian Jonathan Andrews, who has written about the process of discharge at Broadmoor, has talked of the 'sheer amount of work involved in reviewing cases' and says that 'it is the thoroughness and efficiency of the authorities that impresses'.[56] This is borne out by the diligence with which Nicolson approached Mary's case. In June 1887, he received a letter from the Home Office, stating that George would like Mary to be released because he believed 'she is now sane'. (The Home Office letters and responses are all summarized in handwritten documents.) We don't know how George made the representation to the Home Office, or why he thought she was sane – perhaps he had managed to make at least one visit. It seems likely that George was illiterate, so it is possible that this approach, like later ones, was made through the vicar who then approached the local MP. The Home Office repeated the request on 25 February 1888, and on 29 March 1888: the February letter mentions that George 'prays for his wife's release on the ground that he has no one to look after his children'. These letters show that George's MP, the Conservative Frank Hardcastle, has acted as an intermediary.

Hardcastle's intervention may have been helpful. It was common for families to involve clergy and MPs in their appeal for release, and the Home Office 'would look favourably upon an application if it were supported by a person of consequence'.[57] It seems likely that the Frances' Anglicanism made them a particularly sympathetic case in Hardcastle's eyes. Yet Nicolson seems to have preferred to rely on his own judgement: he turned down each of the requests, and in his letter of 22 June 1887, he describes Mary as 'still insane and quite unfit to be discharged'.

Broadmoor sent annual patient reports to the Home Secretary, and the report on Mary dated 10 December 1888 represents a turning point. The cause of Mary's insanity – previously unidentified – is now confidently described as 'hereditary and puerperal'. Her bodily health is 'much improved' while her mental condition is 'much improved but not yet fully recovered'.

Over the next two years her notes read:

- 21st Dec '89 Going on quietly and well in Ward 3. Working in the scullery, is cheerful and contented looking.
- 21st Feb '90 No change to record. Works well in scullery Wd 3. Cheerful looking. Salutes with a meaningless inane smile. Her ordinary mental condition, in which she apparently now is, was never at its best very strong.

- 16th April '90 A woman of originally weak mind. Suffers from goitre.
- 30th June '90 Her mental condition improves. She is hardworking, well conducted, though being somewhat deaf makes her appear to be more stupid than she really is.

Poor Mary: Graves' disease no doubt had an impact on her physical health, her mental state and her cognitive function, and the trauma of knowing that she had killed her own child must have been profound. Nonetheless she was clearly improving: in 1891 her notes describe her as 'mentally brighter and more cheerful' and in 1892 as 'orderly, rational, industrious and well conducted'.

By 1891, George was living in Shuttle Street, Hindley, with his three surviving children, now aged 15, 10 and 7. Joseph was working as a drawer in the coal mine. Once again, the Frances were relying on the support of wider family, in the shape of two nieces, Sarah and Harriet Garside, aged 24 and 22 respectively, who lived with them. Although their jobs are recorded in the census as general servants, it seems likely they were also helping to look after the younger children.

That same year George again petitioned for Mary to be released. A letter from the Home Office dated 3 November 1891 says that Hardcastle has forwarded a letter from the Reverend H. H. Oliver, applying for Mary's release. Oliver was the first vicar of St James's Church in Daisy Hill, Westhoughton, built in 1881.[58] He had apparently been in communication with Broadmoor, and told Hardcastle that 'the doctor and matron both report her [Mary] well enough to be released'. For George, the laborious process of having to go through the vicar, who in turn had to approach the MP, who then had to ask the Home Office to write to Broadmoor, must have been wearing; but it is testimony to the persistence of Hardcastle and Oliver – and perhaps to a belief in George's good character – that they were willing to act repeatedly on his behalf. The draft of Nicolson's reply, dated 12 November 1891, caustically states that Oliver has 'somewhat overstated the case and thereby caused some amount of misapprehension to arise in Mr Hardcastle's mind'. He goes on:

> No doubt 'the doctor and the matron' spoke in most favourable terms of Mrs France's mental condition and character; but my colleague did not without qualification say that he 'saw no reason why she should not return home' (if he used these words at all). The result of the Clergyman's statement has, apparently, been to make Mr Hardcastle believe that the S of S [superintendent of staff] detains Mrs France in custody against the testimony from Broadmoor and this clearly is not so. It would perhaps be well if this were explained to Mr Hardcastle.
>
> It would be an unkindness to Mrs France and to her husband and family to send her home while any reasonable ground of risk remained whereby a relapse into insanity might be caused.

This firmness in the face of external pressure is no doubt a mark of Nicolson's integrity – but probably also represents a desire to make a show of his medical authority.

In his study of the process of discharging child-murderers from Broadmoor and Perth Criminal Lunatic Department, Jonathan Andrews notes that the factors taken into account included the patient's level of education, her family's level of education, the family's willingness to receive her back and whether she had been through the menopause.[59] Women were regarded as mentally frail, with their minds to some extent influenced by the changes in their bodies. In Mary's case, the menopause initially delayed her discharge, because it was regarded as a time when women could lapse again into insanity – though once menopause was over, the removed risk of pregnancy meant that women were thought less likely to relapse.[60]

In November 1891, when Mary was 44, a draft letter from Nicolson to the Home Office states that

> the critical period of female life at which she has arrived has made a postponement of her release desirable. After the lapse of another period of 6 months this difficulty may no longer exist and she will very possibly be fit for release, if application is made by the husband.

He asks the Home Office to pass on a message to Hardcastle that Mary is not well enough to be released but that George should make another application in six months' time.

The Home Office's final application for Mary's release was made on 14 May 1892. By now her bodily health was 'good' and her state of mind 'rational, tranquil, orderly and industrious'. At the end of September 1892, Mary was issued with a warrant of conditional release into the care of her husband, who was living at No. 1 Deansgate, Hindley, near Wigan. Mary had been in Broadmoor for five and a half years, a slightly shorter stay than average.

George seems to have fulfilled his duty to report on Mary's condition every three months conscientiously. In a letter dated April 1893, he wrote (or someone wrote for him) asking whether he needed to send a doctor's certificate or should wait for the form to arrive. He added that Mary was 'quite well and hearty'. A handwritten note underneath states that a form was to be sent and returned 'unless he shall have cause to report any unfavourable symptoms in his wife's condition, in which case of course he would report without any delay'. After many years of separation from her family, Mary must have been delighted to see her own mother again, but heartbreakingly, she wasn't able to spend very much time with her: Jane died in 1893, aged 68. Four years later, Mary's younger sister, Nancy, died, aged only 42.

After that, there are no more records of the Frances' interactions with Broadmoor. In 1901, George and Mary were no longer living in Hindley. They had moved to 20, Warrington Road in nearby Ince, Makerfield, where they lived with their daughter Jane, now 17 and working as an apprentice milliner – a step up socially for the France family. Mary's eldest son James was married with three children of his own, but tragedy was to strike again: James was killed in a pit accident at Garswood Hall Colliery, caused by a fall of roofing, in June 1908. He was 39.

It was probably James's death, which left his 39-year-old widow Nancy to bring up three children alone, that caused a change in the Frances' living arrangements. Mary moved in with her adult daughter Betsy Smith, her husband William (a painter in a colliery) and their young son Albert. The house they lived in, 14 Bickershaw Lane, Abram, was a small, redbrick end of terrace, and is still there today. George moved in with the widowed Nancy, who lived with her children Albert, Florice and Harry at 239, Bryn Road, Ashton in Makerfield. George was working as a 'dataller' in a coal mine – this meant that he was hired on a daily basis, a more precarious and worse-paid living even than piece work.[61] It's possible that poverty had driven Mary and George to move in with other people, or perhaps Nancy needed George's income to support her. It may even be the case, though it seems unlikely, that George and Mary were temporarily estranged.

If so, they got back together and stayed together till the end. Both George and Mary ended up living with Betsy at a new address in Abram, 77, Warrington Road. George was to die in February 1923, at the age of 71, of cerebral thrombosis, or brain haemorrhage, but with bronchopneumonia, a lung disease common in coal miners, given as a secondary cause. Mary followed a year later, in March 1924, aged 77, dying of myocardial degeneration, a broad term for heart disease. She left effects of £123 18s 7d.

Mary's life was an ordinary one made extraordinary by a single, terrible crime. Her day-to-day existence before she killed her baby daughter was characterized by features common to working-class Lancashire women in the mid- to late nineteenth century: poverty, hard work, repeated childbearing and infant mortality. Yet the response to her crime illustrates the relatively benign – if paternalistic – attitudes of the authorities towards women who killed their children in an act of insanity. It's an attitude we can see in the kindness of police towards her, in the testimony of the medical witnesses, in the direction of the judge to the jury and in the support of the local vicar and MP petitioning for her release. She also benefitted from the close-knit family ties that remained characteristic of working-class life in the industrial era: despite the shocking nature of her crime, she did not lose the support of her mother, husband or children.

Perhaps most strikingly, although she was poor and uneducated, in the eyes of her contemporaries, Mary's defining quality was her 'respectability': it was this respectability, demonstrated in part through a strong sense of religious obligation, that drew sympathy, rather than judgement, from her community; respectability that led to a detention in Broadmoor rather than a prison sentence; and respectability that helped her to a relatively early release.

Chapter 3

Mary Ann Meller

Mary Ann Neal was born in Southwark, South London, and, aside from her time in Broadmoor, spent her whole life there. Southwark is one of the areas of London that has, as one writer puts it, 'existed and thrived since medieval times as a result of its proximity to London Bridge'.[1] It was a place that had always bustled with markets and traders, but its status as a centre of business became even more pronounced in the nineteenth century when the industrial revolution saw London become the world's largest port.

Queen Victoria came to the throne in 1837: Mary Ann was born just three years later in the parish of St Saviour. This was an area rich in history – Shakespeare himself lived there for ten years, lodging for a while on Silver Street while his plays were performed in Southwark's Globe Theatre. It was also home to Borough Market and St Saviour's Church, later to become Southwark Cathedral.

Mary grew to adulthood at a time when Southwark was changing rapidly. The building of Waterloo Bridge in 1817 and Southwark Bridge in 1819, followed by the opening of the London Bridge railway terminus in 1836, brought a good deal of new trade, and Southwark's population nearly doubled between 1801 and 1851. Despite being a centre of wealth creation, it was also one of the poorest areas of London, its residents living in cheap, overcrowded housing, with multiple families sharing a single outdoor toilet. Houses close to the river were regularly flooded, and diseases such as measles and pneumonia were rife. The Thames, which was the main source of drinking water for London's residents, was regularly contaminated by sewage, leading to four cholera epidemics in the capital, in 1832, 1848, 1853 and 1866. In 1851, when the journalist Henry Mayhew published his book on London's poor, he identified Southwark as one of the places worst affected by the 1848 cholera outbreak: the 'capital of cholera', he wrote, was Jacob's Island, to the east of St Saviour's dock.[2]

The social reformer Charles Booth also believed St Saviour's to be one of the poorest places in London, something borne out by the high mortality rate: in the 1860s, only 50 per cent of children born in St Saviour's would reach their fifth birthday.[3] Pubs were plentiful and drunkenness common.[4] This was particularly true on a Saturday night, with fights frequently breaking out on the street and in families.[5] Perhaps surprisingly, crime rates were comparatively low: people would leave their front doors open and hang their washing out in the street.[6]

Mary Ann's family were better off than the bulk of Southwark residents. Her father, James Neal, had been born in Lingfield in Surrey in about 1815, and had married Mary Gorringe, who came from East Grinstead, in 1834. James was young – only 19 at the time of the marriage, while Mary was 25. Their first child, John, was born a year later and their second, James, in 1838.

James's parents, John and Elizabeth, had married in December 1814 while Elizabeth was pregnant with him. At the time of his birth, his father was a labourer – yet much later, he was to enjoy relative prosperity as a farmer. It's not impossible that this is related to the success of James's own business as a coal merchant: perhaps James was able to help his father out financially. This is all speculative, however. Whatever the case, James seems to have remained close to his parents – certainly at the time of the 1851 census, the boys were staying with their grandparents at Coventry Farm in Hendon. According to this census (not always a reliable source), John was farming 300 acres and employing four labourers – a very small number for such a large farm. Much later, after Elizabeth's death, John came to live with James and Mary.

In the early days of marriage, the family lived in Albion Place (now Heygate Street), and James worked as coal carman – someone employed by a coal merchant to deliver coal to people's houses.

Coal was a central part of London's economy, with 3.5 million tons brought by ship to the city's docks each year from the northern coalfields.[7] (Later in the century much of the coal was transported by rail.) It was also an ubiquitous part of Victorian life, used for domestic fires and industrial fuel alike. As we have already seen, soot from coal went everywhere, covering interiors with a thin layer of grime, while the smoke from kitchen ranges and fireplaces 'together with London's foggy climate, ensured that London was filthy, inside and out'.[8] A rather florid contemporary account of the carman's job described his role as bearing into the streets 'luxuries for which the ocean has been ploughed', adding: 'No marvel that with such a trust he walks erect, carries his whip somewhat jauntily, and looks with a proud eye at his horses – subjects who obey his very nod, and, unlike the human wicked world, never entertain a thought of dethroning him.'[9] Although overwritten, it gives a sense of just how important coal was to London's life. It was a very good business for James to be in.

By the time Mary Ann was 11, James was a coal merchant himself, employing 34 men and boys, making the family relatively affluent. They had moved from Albion Place to 17, Cross Street in Bermondsey before moving again to Old Jamaica Wharf, a large riverside building sited at 1, Upper Ground Street in Southwark, the road where you'll find the South Bank Centre today. The Neals' eldest child, John, had died of measles in 1843, aged only 7. James and Mary Ann, however, were soon joined by two more siblings: Thomas in 1845 and Emma in 1847. Their parents had enough money to send the children to school, where they learnt to write: Mary Ann's admission form to Broadmoor described her education as 'good', a rarity amongst the female patients. (Her own mother was illiterate, signing the marriage register with a cross.)

Both she and Thomas, however, showed signs of mental illness from childhood. Mary Ann's mother was described at trial as 'very weak in mind', and Thomas was said to have been 'all his life subject to insanity'. In 1863, he was admitted to Camberwell Asylum on Peckham Road (referred to at trial as 'Dr. Pond's Lunatic Asylum'). While still at school, Mary Ann left a letter to her parents on the table, saying that she had killed herself. They searched for her all day up and down the river, but couldn't find her, and at night she returned unharmed.

James, now the eldest of the four remaining children, was the first to leave home. He travelled to Victoria, Australia – a sea journey that could take months – where in 1856 he married Bridget Cleary, an Irishwoman, who had been born in Newagh, Tipperary. Their first child, Mary Ann, was born two years later in Ballarat, Victoria. What took Bridget and James to Australia – and how they met – is probably destined to remain a mystery. But they came back to Southwark and set up home at 38, New Cut (these days known as The Cut), and James took up employment working as a clerk for his father. Their daughter was soon joined by Elizabeth, Emma and John – all Neal family names. Within a few years they were able to afford to keep a domestic servant.

On 2 July 1859, Mary Ann married William Meller (sometimes spelt Mellor or even Miller) at Christ Church, Southwark, an Anglican church built in 1671. William, who lived just a mile away from the Neal family home, at 15, Trinity Square, was fourteen years older than Mary Ann. He worked as a self-employed stonemason, a skilled manual job that typically involved building, or repairing, monuments, gravestones and ornamental structures. As would have been usual at the time, William was a member of the United Grand Lodge of Freemasons.

William was following in the footsteps of his father John Meller, also a stonemason. Although he had been born in Gawber, Yorkshire, it seems very likely that William moved to London for work: as

London grew rapidly, the need for craftsmen and builders increased, and the advent of the railways had reduced journey times between Yorkshire and London to just a few hours. The job put William in what the Victorians called the 'artisan' class – newspaper reports of Mary Ann's trial were to describe him as a 'respectable tradesman', and in Mary Ann's Broadmoor file he was referred to as 'well to do'.

One nineteenth-century stonemason, Henry Broadhurst, has left us an account of his working life. His father was also a stonemason, and Broadhurst thought that 'most lads will learn their father's trade quicker than any other'.[10] He seems for the most part to have enjoyed his work, and he worked on many of the best-known buildings in London, including Westminster Abbey, the Albert Hall and St Thomas's Hospital. The job wasn't always easy, however, often requiring long hours out of doors in all weathers. Describing his work on the clock tower (Big Ben) next to the Houses of Parliament, Broadhurst writes that the 'north-east wind blowing up the river made my task a cruel one. At times the bitter blast would numb my hands until it was impossible to hold a chisel'.[11]

The couple's first child, Rosetta, was born on 7 December 1860, and on 27 January the following year, she was baptized at the same church where her parents were married. For a while at least, Mary Ann and William continued to live with her parents at Old Jamaica Wharf. When the 1861 census was taken, it was a full house. As well as being home to James and Mary (now aged 45 and 50), William, Mary Ann and baby Rosetta, the occupants included Mary Ann's younger brother and sister – 16-year-old Thomas, now working as a clerk to a coal merchant (almost certainly his father) and 14-year-old Emma, who was employed as a domestic servant. They also had a family of boarders in the house: husband and wife Nathaniel and Mary Pickett, and their children Robert (6) and John (5), as well as another boarder, 66-year-old widower John Ormond, a candlemaker. James's coal merchant business was flourishing: he now employed sixty-one men and seven boys.

After her marriage, Mary Ann once more began displaying symptoms of insanity. One of these symptoms, according to her Broadmoor file, was that she defaced her husband's portrait, though this could surely just have been an expression of rage during a disagreement. It can't have helped that for several years she was either pregnant or breastfeeding. Rosetta's birth in 1860 was followed by three more in rapid succession: William (1862), Charles (1863) and Selina (1864). She also suffered several miscarriages. Once more she tried to kill herself, travelling to Cheam, eleven miles away, for that purpose. Arriving at midnight, she was found and brought home at 4 am.

At some point, Mary Ann began drinking. The problem of excessive drinking in women was a major concern in the Victorian era and, as we saw earlier, it was a particular problem in Southwark with its bigger-than-average share of pubs. Charles Booth, who mapped the lives of the London poor, interviewed the police, the clergy, schoolmasters and others about women's drinking habits, who all largely agreed that the increase in drinking was a by-product of women's greater financial independence. One of his interviewees told Booth: 'Public-houses are more attractive than they were; ladies' saloon bars are to be seen everywhere. Publicans tell you that it is in response to a demand, but it is difficult to distinguish between cause and effect.'[12]

Several commented that drinking was more common amongst married women than single, with one saying: 'Factory girls drink, but it is more often the young married women and the middle-aged who indulge too much. Men drink beer; women more often spirits. Women drink more than they used to, perhaps because they earn more.'

One question we can't know the answer to is whether Mary Ann's bouts of mental illness were caused by her drinking, or whether the mental illness led her to self-medicate (to use a modern term) with alcohol.

Mary Ann's mental illness was most apparent during her confinements. At her trial for assault in 1868, her doctor, William

Randle, was to testify that he had known her for eight years. During that time either he or his assistants had tended her when she was giving birth or miscarrying, and he told the court that when she was mentally ill, she was 'in a state utterly beyond self-control'. At some point, she even tried to kill her husband. James continued to see his daughter every week, and worried, he later testified, that she would kill either William or one of the children.

As well as the stress of childbearing, Mary Ann was struck by two tragedies in rapid succession: her younger brother Thomas died of tuberculosis in 1866, followed by her sister Emma, who died of the same disease in 1867. Both were only 20. Tuberculosis (known popularly as 'consumption') was a major scourge of the Victorian era, killing four million people in England and Wales between 1851 and 1910. A highly contagious disease that spread quickly in overcrowded cities, it was most commonly found in the lungs, though it could attack any part of the body. People with tuberculosis of the lungs would typically grow feverish and pale, lose weight and cough up blood. It appears on the death certificates of many of the people featured in this book.

Early in 1867, Mary Ann was once again displaying symptoms of mental illness and tried to kill herself by taking ammonia. A doctor was called in and persuaded her with difficulty to take an antidote. (In reality, Mary Ann must have recovered spontaneously – there is no effective antidote to ammonia.)

By this time, Mary Ann and William were living in 20, St George's Road, in the area known as Elephant and Castle. Later that year, Mary Ann was once again pregnant and clearly mentally unwell. Randle told William that she was not safe to be at liberty and recommended putting her in an asylum. William was particularly worried, given her history, that she would hurt either him or the children. Before he could find an asylum to house Mary Ann, however, he hired a widow named Mary Cattermole as a live-in carer – variously described as aged 64, 68 and 70 in newspaper reports. Mrs Cattermole had known the Mellers for seven years, and had also attended Mary Ann in childbirth. At these times, Mrs Cattermole was later to tell a jury, Mary Ann had 'suffered terribly' and after giving birth had been 'out of her mind'.

On 1 November 1867, Mary Ann came to Mrs Cattermole's room between 6 am and 7 am and told her that William was coming home to have his breakfast. Mrs Cattermole went to the kitchen and began laying a wood fire. Unaware that anyone else was in the kitchen, she suddenly received a 'dreadful blow' on her head. She sat down on a chair, placed her hand on her head and then taking it away saw that it was covered in blood. She told the Old Bailey trial, held on 16 December, what happened next:

> The prisoner was then at the table, she came before me and cut me across the throat, and said, 'What is that, Mrs. Cattermole?' I said, 'Oh murder!' She then cut me on the other side. I went to get the kitchen door open but found it was fastened – she pulled my hair and said, 'You don't go alive.' She turned round to get the broom, and I got to the street door and found the chain up. She tore my hair – I got out of the house into the street, and was taken to a surgeon's and from there to the hospital. My hand was also wounded when I put it up to save my throat'.

With some understatement, she concluded: 'I considered the prisoner very odd at times.'

The wounds were 'severe' (Mary Ann had cut her throat with a razor), and Mary Cattermole had to be taken by two men to nearby Guy's Hospital for treatment. It took her several weeks to recover. A passing policeman, Theophilus Mason, asked them what happened, and hurried to the house where he found Mary Ann in a passage being held by two men, and that she was 'in anything but a rational state'. Mason found the razor, still covered in blood, on the kitchen mantelpiece. Blood was also on the floor and the dresser. Mary Ann immediately admitted to the crime. According to the newspaper report, paraphrasing Mason's evidence: 'She said directly he entered the house, "I have cut Mrs Cattermole's throat with a razor." She said she was very sorry and hoped she had not injured the old lady much. She repeated this incoherently all the way to the station.'[13]

Later that day, Mary Ann appeared at Southwark Police Court (what we would now call a magistrates' court), charged with attempted murder. She was remanded to the infirmary of Horsemonger Lane gaol where she stayed until her Old Bailey trial.[14]

Horsemonger gaol is worth a small detour. One of several prisons in Southwark, also known as Surrey County gaol, Horsemonger was a three-storey building, used to detain both prisoners and debtors after the notorious debtors' prison, Marshalsea, closed in 1842. The journalist and reformer Henry Mayhew had described Horsemonger in 1862 as 'inclosed within a dingy brick wall, which almost screens it from the public eye'. He noted the 'staircase leading up to a gloomy chamber, containing the scaffold on which many a wretched criminal has been consigned to public execution'.

Indeed, Horsemonger was the site of many public executions: in 1849, Charles Dickens attended the hanging of two people, a couple known as the Mannings, who had been convicted of murdering a friend for his money. In a letter to *The Times*, Dickens gave a horrified account of their deaths, and the response of the crowd who treated the executions as entertainment, which led to public executions being abolished in 1868.[15]

While at Horsemonger, Mary Ann was well behaved. The governor, John Keene, described her as 'quiet and well conducted betraying no symptoms of insanity'. (Keene had his own, extraordinary, sad story: his son, also John, was hanged at the gaol for murdering his wife's illegitimate child in 1852.)[16]

At her Old Bailey trial, Dr Randle testified that Mary Ann's bout of insanity was a result of the 'frequency of having children and the frequency of miscarriages'. He said that in some women there was a 'tendency to destroy even their own children' and that he had seen a woman 'throw her infant to the other side of the room'. Asked by Mary Ann's defence lawyer about puerperal mania, he said that, in his view, 'there is another condition in which a person is in a very low, weak state; that is connected with suckling, and that is her state – I am of the opinion that she suffers from intermittent insanity.' He added that in Mary Ann's case, the crime was 'an impulse perfectly beyond her control'. Once again, the medical view was not that the defendant was incapable of understanding what she had done (in line with the McNaughton rule), but that she was incapable of preventing herself from doing it.

Mary Ann was found not guilty on the grounds of insanity. When she arrived at Broadmoor, she was only 27 years old and already the mother of four children, the youngest of whom was 3. She was seven months pregnant.

Her patient case file has a picture of Mary Ann, dated 'Broadmoor, 1867'. (We do not have permission to reproduce it here.) In it, she is seated stiffly on a hard chair, dressed very formally in an elegant gown that appears to be a crinoline, with a sash bound tightly at the waist. She has a full face, and wears her hair plaited over her head. She looks every inch a respectable, middle-class Victorian woman, betraying no sign of either drunkenness or insanity.

On the Schedule A transfer form from Horsemonger to Broadmoor, Keene described Mary Ann's bodily health as 'good – pregnant'. He admitted that the cause of insanity was 'not known'. Under the question about whether she was 'of temperate habits' Keene has written 'said not to be', which was all too true. In response to the question of whether she was suicidal or dangerous to others, he wrote: 'Yes, yes.' He recorded that Mary Ann's keep while at Broadmoor was to be paid for by her local parish, St Mary Newington, to the sum of fourteen shillings a week.

Mary Ann gave birth to her fifth child, Henry, on 18 March. Henry was healthy, and his mother produced enough milk to feed him. After three weeks – on 9 April – William came to Broadmoor and collected him. (Others who gave birth at Broadmoor were not so lucky: one woman, Margaret Crimmings, with no husband to look after her child, had her baby daughter taken away after a few weeks to a workhouse, where she died.)

Over time, Mary Ann's behaviour improved. In April, staff recorded that she required 'careful watching' because she had a 'violent temper' and had pulled a nurse's cap off. But by July, Mary Ann was described as being 'in excellent health'. She was sleeping and eating well, 'free from any known delusion … cheerful and well conducted, employed at needlework'. More concerning, however, was the statement that she 'does not appreciate her position or the offence which brought her here. Speaks of her trouble but in a casual manner'. By October, her manner was described as 'quiet and self satisfied' but 'irritable when opposed'. She no longer showed any signs of delusion, but 'is stated to have been of intemperate habits when there was opportunity'.

If Mary Ann was mostly quiet and well behaved, the rest of Broadmoor was experiencing an eventful year. One male patient, JP, attempted suicide by cutting his leg and arm with a concealed piece of crinoline steel. One of the staff, principal attendant Dobson, was diagnosed with heart disease, left his job and died shortly afterwards. For three years he had been in charge of a block occupied by 'violent and dangerous men', and the superintendent, John Meyer thought that the 'anxious nature of this service induced the disease which cost him his life'. The deputy superintendent, William Orange, was struck by two male patients, while EP, a 'female patient of the convict class' had shown herself to be 'violent and dangerous'. EP twice attacked the attendants, and inflicted an 'incised wound' on the forehead of a nurse. On three occasions she also attacked other patients.

Seven patients – six men and one woman – died during the year, from diseases such as cancer, bronchitis and 'disease of brain'. There was also a bout of 'simple continued fever', affecting forty-five patients, thirty-six attendants and twenty-six other people at Broadmoor.

On top of all that, five male patients (four of them convicts) escaped during the year. The superintendent noted that it was particularly difficult preventing convicts from escaping: 'it must be remembered that insanity does not deprive the experienced thief or housebreaker of his craft. It made it harder to treat the lunacy,' he added, because 'one cannot afford to forget the habits and tendencies of the man'.[17]

In his report, the chaplain, J. T. Burt, was similarly disparaging about the convicts transferred from prison. As well as their own 'personal depravity', he wrote, they had been 'taught the worst lessons of prison life' and 'the amount of remaining intelligence possessed by some of them allows of their exerting an injurious influence over others'. In 1868, it seems, Broadmoor was not a happy place. Burt went on:

> It has been my lot for nearly twenty-eight years to labour in asylums and prisons, but it never fell to my lot before to witness depravity and unhappiness in forms so aggravated. In other asylums, when the mind resumes anything like healthy action, there is hope of discharge. In prisons, the period of detention, however long, has some definite duration; but here, the fear of relapse, and the terrible acts to which relapse may lead, render the conditions of release rarely attainable; for many the period of detention is indefinite, and hope is almost excluded.[18]

And yet that proved not to be the case for Mary Ann. She continued to make good progress. In January 1869, she was showing clear signs of recovery, with her manner described as 'subdued'. She was now more 'rational' and speaking of her past. She admitted that when she attacked Mrs Cattermole, it was under the influence of drink taken the previous night. Now, however, free from the temptations of drink, she showed no symptom of insanity. By April the following year she was sleeping well, employed regularly in the workroom and was 'rational and much improved in general appearance and manner'.

In fact, she had improved so much that in May 1870, after only two years as a patient, she was conditionally discharged, and William came to Broadmoor to take her home.

By this time, things had changed for Mary Ann's parents too. James's mother Elizabeth (Mary Ann's grandmother) died in 1870. At about this time, James packed up his coal merchant business, moving with Mary to Horne, in the Surrey countryside, to run a 100-acre farm. James's father John moved in with them. The new rural idyll was short-lived: Mary was widowed in October 1871 when James died of a stroke at the age of 56, leaving effects of nearly £8,000.

By 1871, the Meller family were at a new address: 101, Falmouth Road, half a mile from their old home. As well as the four older children (Rosetta, now 10; William, 8; Charles, 7; and Selina, 6), the family now included Henry, who had been born in Broadmoor, and baby Florence, conceived not long after Mary Ann returned home. Florence and Henry were both baptized on 21 May 1871 at Newington St Matthew – presumably William had not got round to baptizing Henry while Mary was in Broadmoor. The family was wealthy enough to employ a servant, 17-year-old Eliza Scott.

Mary Ann was to give birth two more times: to a boy, James, in early 1874, and to another girl, Emmeline, in 1875. For a woman suffering from mental health problems, known to be exacerbated by birth, the impact of having three more children in the space of five years must have been harsh.

It wasn't long after coming out of Broadmoor that Mary Ann took to drink again.

In February 1873, William wrote to Mrs Jackson, probably the Broadmoor staff member responsible for the female patients, saying that Mary Ann had been drinking heavily in the past four months, and asking for advice. The doctor, he wrote, had told him not to let her have much money, and, as a result, she had begun pawning anything she could to have money for drink. Mary Ann, William wrote, 'goes out of one Public House into another and drinks until she is quite insensible and cannot stand.' That very evening, she had been brought home by a lady who passed their house most days. Recently, he added, Mary Ann had pawned her gold watch and then lost the ticket – which was then sold in a pub in a 'low neighbourhood' a fortnight after it was lost. Fortunately, one of the customers recognized the name on the ticket and reported it to the police, enabling William to retrieve the watch from the pawnbroker. The family, he added, were travelling to the country to visit their eldest daughter (Rosetta), who had been staying with his mother-in-law since Mary Ann's father, James, had died in 1871. (Later, both Charles and Selina were, separately, to spend time at their grandmother's house. Perhaps Mary Neal's mental frailty required her to have a live-in companion taking care of her.)

Unfortunately, Mary Ann pawned the watch again and used the money to buy a pair of earrings. She also bought drink, becoming so tipsy that 'there were a mob of at least a couple of hundred people after her'. Mary Ann had told the family servant that she was planning to attend a lecture. William – accompanied by their church minister – tried to track her down at the lecture, and when this proved futile, went searching in all the public houses. Eventually, giving up, he went into a chemist shop for some pills and told the proprietor, who expressed some concern about his worn-out appearance, that he couldn't find his wife. The letter goes on:

> He then said that a drunken woman had just gone along with a couple of hundred people after her and that there did not appear to be a policeman about the place. My

> heart really appeared as if it was in my mouth, I went out of the shop and looking the way he told me she had gone, and behold there was a mob of the number he had told me. I hastened to the spot and after a great deal of squeezing I ultimately got thro' the mob, and behold my wife in the shop as before described.

A policeman came and cleared the mob away, and William put Mary Ann in a cab. She was unable to sit on the seat, so he had to let her lie down on the bottom of the cab.

William mentions that he is afraid to talk to Mary Ann's mother about her, but adds that the drunkenness is affecting her capacity to look after their children:

> Only on Wednesday last our servant had a holiday and I consequently came home early to Tea on purpose to see how she was getting on, and am sorry to say that she was again quite Tipsy and there was my little girl Selina about seven years of age with the two babies, during the time she was in that state a man brought some coals and had to take them thro' the House. The poor little dear says Papa, I managed to get Mama into the parlour before the Man came in, so that he could not see her. It really seems to make my blood run cold to think of it with a family of seven nice children, a comfortable Home and a wife driving to destruction in this manner.

This passage contains a puzzle. The records show that in 1873, at the time the letter was written, the Mellers had six children, not seven. Selina, who was 8, would have been looking after Henry, aged 4, and Florence, not yet 2. There is no indication in the historical record that Mary Ann gave birth to any more children. So it seems that William, as well as getting Selina's age wrong, miscounted his own children.

William asks Mrs Jackson to write to Mary Ann, as she would be likely to take some notice of her. He concludes by mentioning that it is 2.30 on a Sunday afternoon, and that Mary Ann has been lying on her bed since 8 o'clock: 'I intend not to disturb her but let her wake up and find herself in the bed room alone.'

There is no record of whether Mrs Jackson wrote to Mary Ann, but William wrote again to Broadmoor in April, saying that his wife had been 'more comfortable and settled this last week'. Her medical attendant had not been to see her that week, he added, but William had asked that he visit soon.

Another letter, however, paints a different picture. Undated, it gives us the rare opportunity to hear Mary Ann's voice. In scrawled handwriting, not all of which is legible, Mary Ann writes to William Orange (who had taken over as superintendent on John Meyer's death in 1870):

> Will you kindly call at my house 101 Falmouth Rd as I am miserable & unhappy & require your assistance and as I shall be in receipt of 2 Pounds per week very shortly & Mr Meller threatens to send me away from home & has I believe broken the bone of my nose & blackened my eye, I would rarther [*sic*] be under your care & have be & has ill used my servant informs me [*sic*].
>
> He received a letter from the Secretary of State kindly requesting your attention & I remain yours
>
> Ob[edient]ly M. A. Meller.
>
> If you cannot see me yourself, please send Mrs Anderson as she has [illegible – resided with?] me.

If we are to believe Mary Ann's account, then she was the victim of domestic violence, which would go a long way to explaining her unhappiness. Was William not the caring husband he appeared to be?

Was this the first time he had hit her, perhaps enraged at her habitual drunkenness? Or perhaps Mary Ann's drinking was a response to the misery of living with a domestic abuser? Might Mary Ann have been exaggerating for sympathy? We can't, at this distance, know, but the letter at least suggests an alternative interpretation of events to that of 'concerned husband worried about alcoholic wife'.

William wrote to Orange again in April:

> Mr Orange
> Sir
>
> Mrs Meller seems pretty comfortable. She has been into Lancashire and Yorkshire visiting my Relations and has brought home our little boy Henry, a very fine little fellow, the one that was born in the Asylum. Doctor Randle has not yet returned to business. Has [*sic*] soon as he does he will write to you.
>
> Yours obediently
>
> W. Meller
>
> I am going to take her today to visit my cousin at his country House Lippots Hill Lodge, High Beach.

(Coincidentally, High Beach in Lippitts Hill, Epping Forest, had been a mental asylum between 1825 and 1850. Like Broadmoor, it had been run on progressive lines and was for four years home to the poet John Clare.)

Afterwards, the family moved to 158, New Kent Road – described by nineteenth-century historian Edward Walford as 'a broad and open roadway; it has been lately planted on either side with trees, so that in course of time it will doubtless form a splendid boulevard, of the Parisian type, and one worthy of being copied in many other parts of London'.[19] In happier circumstances, it would have been a lovely place to live.

We learn no more of what happened to Mary Ann until her premature death at the age of 37 on 23 December 1878. Like her brother Thomas and sister Emma, the cause was tuberculosis. She was buried, not with her father and siblings at St Mary the Virgin church in Horne, but at Nunhead Cemetery in Southwark.

Amongst the middle classes, it was usual for families to make out a memorial card about the deceased, which could then be handed out at the end of a funeral, or given to people who could not make it to the funeral. The memorial card would include the name, age, date of death, where the person was buried and a verse of scripture. The card for Mary Ann read:

> In affectionate remembrance of Mary Anne, the beloved wife of William Miller [Meller], who died Dec 23rd 1878.
>
> Aged 37 years.
>
> And was this day interred in the Family Vault at Nunhead Cemetery.

Her last words were:

> My dear husband, I am dying. Pray for me.
> My dear children, Kneel down and pray for me.
> Let these words be placed upon my Grave stone
> I forgive all and ask forgiveness.
> The lord knoweth I have faith in my Redeemer.
> My time hath come.
> I now fly to the arms of Jesus
> Dead. Dead. Dead.

One feels there may have been some poetic licence in the recording of Mary Ann's last words.

That isn't the end of the story, of course. William continued to bring up his large family alone, though he had the help of an elderly housekeeper, Mary Pickering. Later, he took a male lodger, Thomas Taylor. He also seems to have had a close male friend, Henry Bowers, who was a stonemason and probably a colleague. (Henry turns up as a visitor in the 1881, 1891 and 1911 censuses.) William was to stay at the New Kent Road house for the rest of his life, sharing it for some of the time with his unmarried daughters. He died in 1921 at the age of 93, leaving behind the sum of £1,392 15s 4d, equivalent to about £62,000 today.

The eight children had mixed fortunes. Emmeline, the youngest child, died in 1886 at the age of 10, while William, Mary Ann's eldest son, who worked as a stonemason, died in 1893, aged 30. In 1887, Charles married 23-year-old Amelia O'Neal. He later emigrated to the United States, dying in 1920 in Arizona. James moved to Tunbridge Wells, where he worked in an engineering role in the new car industry. He and his wife Ada had three children: Gladys, William and Roy. James died in 1927, still in his early 50s.

In 1907, when Florence was in her 30s, she spent a few weeks in the Southwark Union workhouse: it seems curious that her well-off father was not able to step in and help her out. Later, however, she was released, and lived well into her 80s, though she never married.

Neither Rosetta nor Selina married. Selina, who as an 8-year-old had cared for her two younger siblings while her mother was drunk, lived for a little while with her maternal grandmother as a companion in her home in Blindley Heath. Later, the two sisters chose to live together, sharing a comfortable three-bedroom house in Twickenham. Rosetta died in 1941, but Selina outlived them all, finally giving up the ghost in 1963 at the age of 98.

Henry, the baby born in Broadmoor in 1868, became a stonemason, like his father, and was married twice. The first time was in 1912 to Ada Elizabeth Harris, who died in 1918, and the second to Rosie

Bennett in 1926. Despite his inauspicious start as an asylum baby, Henry too lived a long life, dying in Kent at the age of 83.

Unlike many of the women in this book, Mary Ann's life was not blighted by poverty, but she was trapped in other ways. She spent much of her 20s pregnant or breastfeeding, compelled to bear child after child, despite the deleterious effect of childbirth on her mental health. The close ties to her birth family may have eased the pain of an unhappy marriage – but in the end, no one was able to save her.

Chapter 4

Elizabeth White

The life of Elizabeth Lyddiatt (sometimes spelt Lydiatt or Lydeatt) was marked by tragedy early. Her 27-year-old mother, Sarah, died of pneumonia just two weeks after Elizabeth's second birthday.

Sarah Gould was born in 1825 in Aldridge in Staffordshire, and she married George Lyddiatt in September 1850. Both were Catholics, and married in the Catholic chapel of Saints Peter and Paul in Wolverhampton. This chapel, built in 1826, was one of the first to be established in England after an Act of 1791 ended the ban on Catholic places of worship.[1] (Both Sarah and George had been baptized in the Church of England, a common practice at a time when there were few Catholic churches.)

George, also born in 1825, came originally from Pebworth in Gloucestershire. At the time of the marriage, and indeed for the rest of his working life, he was a porter to a corn dealer. Elizabeth arrived on 3 August 1851, and was baptized a week later in the same church in which her parents had married.

Elizabeth was George's and Sarah's only child, but in 1856, the motherless Elizabeth acquired a stepmother when George married 31-year-old Susan Hubrey, from Codsall in Staffordshire. Susan (also known as Susannah) had been a servant at Sedgley Park School, a private Catholic school for boys in Wolverhampton. Their daughter, Mary Ann, was born in 1858 and baptized at St Patrick's Church. A year later, Elizabeth gained a half-brother when Susan gave birth to William John. Not long after, the family moved to 92, Park Street, where 3-year-old William died of measles.

It was almost certainly work that had brought George to Wolverhampton, situated as it was in the Black Country, the heart of the new industrial Britain. The advent of steam power had had a transformative effect on the landscape: as Hoskins has written, it meant 'a new and intense concentration of large-scale industry and of the labour-force to man it'.[2] At the same time, the arrival of first the canals – which linked Wolverhampton to seventy-three other towns – and then the railways helped the new industries of iron and coal to grow and drew new people to the town: the population grew from 12,565 in 1801 to nearly 50,000 in 1851, the year Elizabeth was born.[3] A German visitor in 1835 wrote: 'As far as the eye can see, all is black, with coal mines and ironworks.'[4]

So Wolverhampton was relatively wealthy – though this didn't usually translate into prosperity for the ordinary people who lived and worked there. Wages remained low until the 1890s, and before then, about three-quarters of the population lived just at or below subsistence level.[5] Most working people lived in poor-quality accommodation rented from private landlords, without proper sanitation.[6] Many lived in slums. As one government report noted in 1842:

> In the small and dirtier streets, at intervals of every eight or ten houses … the great majority are only three feet wide and six feet high … These narrow passages are also the general gutter … having made your way through the passage, you find yourself in a space varying in size with the number of houses, hutches, or hovels it contains. They are nearly all proportionally overcrowded.[7]

As well as being home to numerous new industries, Wolverhampton retained some of its old agricultural heritage, including a corn mill – now powered, of course, by steam. Corn would arrive from the port at Gloucester and then be taken to the corn mill for grinding. George's job as a porter to corn dealers was an unskilled – and arduous –

manual job that involved carrying corn from the warehouse to the market.

The other appealing thing about Wolverhampton, from George's point of view, was that it was home to a substantial Catholic population. Although Catholicism was a minority religion in England, the Catholic population of Wolverhampton grew in the mid-nineteenth century as the town became more industrialized and immigrants fled Ireland's potato famine to take up labouring jobs. Catholic schools and churches were built to accommodate the growing numbers, but this apparently sparked some local resentment – in the year Elizabeth was born there was even a public meeting against 'the very great evil' of Catholicism.[8]

We don't know much about Elizabeth's childhood, but she was able to read and write, so it's possible that she attended one of the handful of local schools recently opened by the Catholic Church. Like other working-class families, the Lyddiatts moved frequently. By the time of the 1871 census, George, Susan and Mary Ann were living in 52, Snow Hill in Wolverhampton. Susan was working as a housekeeper, while 13-year-old Mary Ann was already working as a domestic servant. This particular census raises as many questions as it answers, however. The night of the census, the family were visited by 23-year-old Horace Bolton, a law student and son of an attorney, whose connection to the Lyddiatts is unknown. Of Elizabeth, there is no sign, and no trace of her elsewhere in the census.

In 1881, George and Susan were living in 34, Dudley Street, one of the main streets in the town centre, and George was still working as a porter to two corn-factors (corn dealers). Once more, however, Elizabeth was not at home, and there is no record of her anywhere else in the census. It's possible that she spent some time in London, perhaps in domestic service, which might have been how she met her future husband – but her marriage certificate doesn't record her as having a job, and gives Dudley Street as her address. Mary Ann, now aged 23, was still living with her parents and working as a dressmaker.

She was to marry William Gibney, a carver and gilder, in 1886. Their first child, Sarah, was born in 1887, and they went on to have three sons and two more daughters.

Although we don't know where Elizabeth was in the intervening years, we do know that in June 1882, at the relatively advanced age of 30, she married Joseph White at the Church of Saints Mary and John – a particularly fine building in the Gothic Revival style that had been constructed in the early 1850s in Wolverhampton's Snow Hill area.[9] Joseph was born in Pimlico, South London, in 1853; both his parents, John and Sarah, had been born in Ireland (John in Kildare, and Sarah in Galway) and had moved to England sometime between the birth of their daughter Jane in Dublin in 1844, and the birth of Joseph nine years later – a time when many Irish families fled to England in response to the famine. There was also a younger brother Edward, born in 1858.

John was a butler, and the family lived at 27, Montpelier Place, Knightsbridge, which seems to have been servants' quarters for a nearby wealthy family. They had lived there for more than ten years when Joseph and Elizabeth married. Joseph, who had started working life as a baker's assistant, was now a coachman in South Kensington.

Elizabeth's father, George, and her half-sister Mary Ann were witnesses to the marriage, suggesting that, whatever the reason for her absence from the previous two censuses, she wasn't estranged from her family.

Although coachman was a working-class job, it was an easier life than, say, working as a miner or as a labourer. It also had the perk of free accommodation, and after their marriage, Elizabeth returned to Kensington with Joseph, where they lived at 10, Reece Mews, newly built by the architect Charles Freake. A 'mews' is a cobbled street made up of stables and carriage houses with living quarters above, so that coachmen could be close to their work. Their employer usually lived in the street just behind, in a much grander property. The mews living quarters themselves were fairly basic, usually just two rooms with no window at the rear – the idea being to stop the coachman and his family seeing the employer strolling in the garden. Sometimes a tunnel connected the basement of the employer's house with the stable, so that servants could move quietly and quickly between the two.

Unlike other parts of the country, where working-class housing was geographically segregated from that of the better-off, servants to wealthy London families were in the odd position of living (albeit in cramped conditions) in the swishest parts of the city. In the twentieth century, when the need for stables in central London disappeared, mews properties were converted to houses, and became extremely desirable. The artist Francis Bacon, for example, lived at 7, Reece Mews, and also used it as his studio. The current owner of number 10, the Whites' former home, paid more than £2 million for it in 2014.

As a coachman to a wealthy family, Joseph's job naturally involved driving the family's coach. But not only that, as *Mrs Beeton's Book of Household Management*, published in 1861, explained:

> Besides skill in driving, he should possess a good general knowledge of horses; he has usually to purchase provender, to see that the horses are regularly fed and properly groomed, watch over their condition, apply simple remedies to trifling ailments in the animals under his charge, and report where he observes symptoms of more serious ones which he does not understand. He has either to clean the carriage himself, or see that the stable-boy does it properly.[10]

Mrs Beeton goes into an extraordinary (but no doubt helpful) amount of detail about how to keep a carriage clean (slushing it with clean water, mopping the body with clean water, including the carved work, washing the wheel and using a water-brush for corners where the mop does not penetrate) as well as how to prepare it for use (brushing the linings, beating the cushions, greasing the wheel tyres and tightening the nuts and bolts).

The main job of the coachman, however, was to drive. As Mrs Beeton explains:

> Having, with or without the help of the groom or stable-boy, put his horses to the carriage, and satisfied himself, by walking round them, that everything is properly arranged, the coachman proceeds to the off-side of the carriage, takes the reins from the back of the horses, where they were thrown, buckles them together, and, placing his foot on the step, ascends to his box, having his horses now entirely under control. In ordinary circumstances, he is not expected to descend, for where no footman accompanies the carriage, the doors are usually so arranged that even a lady may let herself out, if she wishes it, from the inside. The coachman's duties are to avoid everything approaching an accident, and all his attention is required to guide his horses.

A coachman will then typically drive at a 'moderate pace of seven or eight miles an hour'. Any slower, she writes, will get the horses into 'lazy and sluggish habits'. Furthermore:

> The true coachman's hands are so delicate and gentle, that the mere weight of the reins is felt on the bit, and the directions are indicated by a turn of the wrist rather than by a pull; the horses are guided and encouraged, and only pulled up when they exceed their intended pace, or in the event of a stumble; for there is a strong though gentle hand on the reins.

As well as being hard work, the job had its dangers: coaches could turn over when overloaded with baggage, and horses were sometimes hard to control. Coachmen sometimes had to drive for long hours in all weathers, including rain, cold and the heat of a hot summer. We don't know how much Joseph might have earned, because wages varied according to the wealth and status of the employer and the experience of the coachman. The typical range was between £25 and £60 a year.[11] At the low end, this was considerably less than a miner, but work as a coachman offered other benefits, notably, the rent-free accommodation – in the form of either a cottage near the house or, as we have seen, a set of rooms above the stables. But there was also a greater stability in the role: many manual jobs were paid at a day rate, and if there was no work that day the worker didn't get paid. A coachman could stay with the same employer for years – as indeed Joseph did.

It wasn't long before the couple started a family. Joseph Edward was born in 1883, followed by George Wilfred in 1884 and Mary Veronica in 1886. Two years later, Elizabeth's stepmother Susan died of heart disease. By the time their fourth child, John Francis, was born on 12 July 1889, the family had moved three miles away to 21, Wimpole Mews in Marylebone. (As with the Reece Mews properties, Wimpole Mews houses were later to become highly sought after – the osteopath Stephen Ward, who played a major role in the Profumo scandal, lived at 17, Wimpole Mews.)

Joseph's affluent employer, a 46-year-old Catholic widow named Marianne Dunn, lived at 79, Harley Street, a beautiful Georgian townhouse that is now home to a private medical clinic. It was just a few doors away from number 73, where the geologist Charles Lyell had once lived, succeeded by William Gladstone, who was there from 1876 to 1882.

When she was only 21, Marianne had married the 47-year-old George Dunn, who died in 1873 at the age of 57, after ten years of marriage. George had huge private wealth, including estates in Northumberland and Berkshire. She now shared the house with her daughter, Elizabeth, a cousin, Miriam Paine, and five servants.

As well as Elizabeth, Marianne had three sons: George, William and Thomas – all, apart from Thomas, had been born in Northumberland.

It was just after John Francis was born that things started to go wrong for Elizabeth. She started to behave strangely. Initially restless at night, she became depressed and rambling, saying first that she was dying, then that the baby was dying. She refused to go out and Joseph had difficulty persuading her to eat. In late September she was placed in Bethnal House, a private lunatic asylum in Cambridge Road (now Cambridge Heath Road), Bethnal Green. It had once had a reputation for neglect and cruelty, but by the time Elizabeth was there, it was considered by the inspectors to be one of the best asylums in the country, clean and well ventilated, with kind and caring staff.[12] There she appeared both depressed and apathetic, taking an interest in nothing and showing a reluctance to answer questions. She also experienced delusions, believing that she was a beggar, that she had no husband, no friends and no money. While there, she attempted suicide by trying to strangle herself. By December she had improved considerably, and was discharged from the asylum at the request of the woman who admitted her. (We don't know who this is.) In fact, the medical officer, John Kennedy Will, felt that she was not well enough to be discharged, but had no authority to keep her there. He told her husband that he should keep someone in constant attendance on her.

In October, a widow named Mary Deeley had joined the household to take care of the four children. Elizabeth returned home on 10 December, still apparently a little strange, but, in Joseph's view, well enough to be at home. Mary continued to look after the children. On the morning of 14 December, Elizabeth appeared depressed, but helped Mary to wash and dress the children. At about 10 o'clock, Joseph went to work. Mary, Elizabeth and the four children were all in the front room, and Elizabeth decided to take the three older children into the sitting room, where it seems the children also slept, leaving Mary with the baby.

Five minutes later, Mary heard screams from the sitting-room. She went to the door but it was fastened shut, so she ran downstairs to the stable to fetch one of the servants, who also failed to open the door. He fetched the butler, William Gibbons, who forced the door open. The sight that met the servants was horrifying. The two boys, Joseph Edward and George Wilfred, were lying side by side in the crib. Elizabeth was leaning on the crib and twisting a dark blue silk handkerchief around George's neck, but, according to Gibbons's own account, with one hand on Joseph's mouth. Gibbons removed first the handkerchief, and then her hand, and saw that Joseph was dead. Initially thinking she had killed both children, he said: 'Good God! They are both dead,' to which Elizabeth replied, 'Yes, they are.'

The police were called, and Inspector George Robson arrived at the house. Here is his account of what happened:

> On the morning of 14th December I went to 21, Wimpole Mews, and in the room upstairs I saw the dead body of the boy Joseph Edward White; the doctor had been there and had left. I told the prisoner I was a police officer, and should take her into custody for causing the death of her son Joseph Edward White by strangling him with a handkerchief. She said, 'Yes, I know all about it,' and after a pause she said, 'If I had not been interrupted I would have finished the four.' She then in a rambling manner accused her husband of having kept her eleven weeks in an asylum. She looked very wild, and her eyes glared; I put her in a cab and took her to the station. On the way she asked me several times if the other boy would recover. I said I thought he would. She said she hoped he would not, as there was nothing for him or the others to live for. At the station when charged she made no reply; she simply bowed.[13]

A local doctor was also called to the scene, where he witnessed Joseph's body. He later carried out a post mortem and found that the cause of death was suffocation.

After her arrest, Elizabeth was taken to Holloway Prison. The prison, which had been built in 1852, still took both men and women (though in separate wings), and it didn't become women-only until 1902.[14]

When she arrived, she was dejected, staring at the ground, and answered questions put to her by the medical officer, Philip Gilbert, only reluctantly. At her Old Bailey trial, Gilbert testified about the conversation they had:

> She told me she had done this. She wanted her children to go out of the world as there was no one to look after them, because she intended suicide. She said she was afraid of poverty, and that she had been very wicked. She was very restless and sleepless, and she was continually repeating to herself, 'It is quite true.' Eventually she expressed sorrow for what she had done. She used to sob very bitterly at times for hours together, and was in a very depressed and melancholy state. She has improved now. I spoke to her about her children. She gave me the impression of being a devoted mother to her children.

Gilbert and Will agreed that Elizabeth was in a deranged state of mind and not responsible for her actions on the day of the murder. The judge, Mr Justice Hawkins, directed the jury to find her guilty but insane.

At Broadmoor, where Elizabeth was admitted in January 1890, the cause of her insanity was recorded as childbirth. On admission she was dejected, stared at the ground and answered questions reluctantly. In her notes she is described as a 'fairly respectable looking woman with a wild restless expression' and 'very melancholic, strongly suicidal and filled with remorse at the terrible position she is in and the crime she has committed'. It was decided that she would sleep in the infirmary ward where she could be carefully looked after.

Elizabeth was one of fourteen women and forty-six men admitted in 1890. Broadmoor had grown considerably since its early days. At the end of the year, it had 624 patients of whom 150 were women, and the report from the Commissioners of Lunacy, while finding the asylum to be in 'excellent order', also thought it was getting 'very full' and thought it might be necessary to add some accommodation, especially on the female side. The commissioners also received 'no serious complaint' from any of the patients and observed that 'many are very intelligent and manifest no insanity in casual conversation; and there are some who, if they were not criminals, would probably be considered fit for discharge'.[15]

The vast majority were 'pleasure' patients (detained at Her Majesty's Pleasure) rather than convicts, and most of those (322) had committed homicide. That year, twenty-eight patients died, mostly of neurological illnesses or heart disease. A male patient committed suicide, slashing his own throat with a sharpened piece of tin – only the second suicide in the asylum since it was opened. There was also a flu epidemic that year, affecting more than 200 patients, three of whom died from the illness. The epidemic taxed the asylum's resources to the full, with twenty-five of the eighty-four male attendants off duty at one point. Annual leave had to be stopped, along with the outside working parties. A further epidemic, this time of measles, meant that the school had to be closed in the later parts of the year. (The school was for the children of the servants, though from time to time Broadmoor did admit a small number of child patients.) Fortunately, there were no successful escapes that year, and only one incident of serious violence, when a patient assaulted an attendant who fell and fractured his arm.

Although Elizabeth remained melancholy, her spirits did gradually improve. In March 1890 she 'woke a little brighter though still very melancholic and depressed. Her general health has much improved, takes her food better and sleeps better'. By August the same year she is 'much the same, slowly improving from the melancholic condition in which she was on reception' and by November she 'has very much improved since last note. Is much more cheerful and disposed to employ herself'. At about this time, Elizabeth's father died, though this isn't mentioned in her Broadmoor notes. By January 1891 she was so much better that her notes describe her as 'cheerful, rational and contented'. In December 1891, her notes record that she 'writes cheerful and pleasant letters to her husband. Her conduct is good and her mental condition improved'. After that time, reports continue to describe her using words such as 'cheerful,' 'rational' and 'tranquil'.

By this time, Joseph's employer, Marianne Dunn, had moved to Maidenhead in Berkshire, where in 1891 she was living with her two adult sons, 26-year-old George, who had inherited his father's fortune, and 23-year-old William, a colonial merchant. (William was later to marry and move to Chelmsford, while younger brother Tom became a priest. George's sister Elizabeth married a landowner named John Eyston, and they had one daughter, Mary. Elizabeth was widowed relatively young, but survived into her 80s.) Joseph followed her there: after the terrible tragedy of young Joseph's death, it must have felt like a small stroke of good fortune, because it meant the family were now only a few miles from Broadmoor. It did, however, mean leaving behind Joseph's parents, who still lived in the Knightsbridge house where Joseph had been brought up.

Woolley Hall, where the Dunns lived, was an extremely grand country house built in 1780, and George Dunn himself was an amateur scientist, with expertise in astronomy, arboriculture and horology. He was also a noted collector of antique books – his library contained an extensive and valuable collection of early English law books, medieval manuscripts, early printed editions and stamped bindings. The Whites lived in a cottage attached to the stables. (As with their earlier homes, the property has since been converted to a very attractive mews house.)

Dunn, having been born in Newcastle, was educated first in Beaumont College in Windsor and then at Stonyhurst. He had moved to Woolley Hall in 1886. He died of pneumonia in 1912 at the age of only 47. His younger brother Tom officiated at his mass. After extolling his extensive knowledge of multiple subjects, his *Times* obituary said of him:

> With these and other interests and pursuits George Dunn lived a tranquil and sequestered life, unmarried and alone in a large house, where he occasionally entertained one or other of the small band of intimates to whom he was devoted and by whom he was beloved. Neatly dressed, shy, spare, and rather below the middle height, he might sometimes be seen entering the British Museum or the Bodleian Library, or quietly turning over the book-treasures in the London sale rooms. But he never attended meetings or went into society, or gave the smallest encouragement to mere acquaintances. He was a Conservative in politics, a model landlord, and a loyal son of the Catholic Church.[16]

He seems, too, to have been a sympathetic employer. Elizabeth's case, like Mary France's, shows the value of patronage when it came to dealing with the authorities. In the same way that George France was able to enlist the help of his local vicar and MP, Joseph appealed for help from Dunn – and Broadmoor officials were more likely to take note of a wealthy gentleman than of a coachman. Keen to have Elizabeth home, Joseph wrote to Broadmoor to ask if she could be discharged. In September 1894, David Nicolson, the superintendent who succeeded William Orange, wrote a note:

> This is really only her 1st attack, as she was removed from the asylum before recovery. Her husband is a very respectable man and anxious to get her back. Mr Dunn in whose service he is takes much interest in Mrs White

> and promised to look after her welfare. I think that her case might receive favourable consideration and that no unwarranted risk would be in permitting her to return to the care of her husband, Joseph White, Woolley Hall Stables, Maidenhead, on the usual conditions.

Woolley Hall, with its lovely setting, would have provided a very calming environment for Elizabeth to come home to, and she was discharged in 1894. During those few years, her children would have changed considerably: John, a baby when Elizabeth was sent to Broadmoor, was now 5. The family were still there in 1901, by which time George, now 16, was working as a footman, while Mary, 15, was an apprentice dressmaker. John, now 11, was probably at school.

There is no happy ending for Elizabeth, however. At about 8 o'clock on the evening of Friday, 2 May 1902, she told Joseph she was going for a 'blow' (i.e. a walk). Joseph promised to join her in a few minutes after he'd completed a task, but when he went to look for her on the main road, he couldn't find her. He spent the night and the early hours of the morning searching for her. At 4 o'clock he arrived at the town hall where he heard two policemen talking about a woman's body that had been found on the railway line, and realized it must be Elizabeth. The body, terribly mutilated, had been found by the driver of a goods train, who then reported it to the foreman-porter at Maidenhead Station.

The inquest into her death was told that since her discharge from Broadmoor seven years earlier, she had appeared 'quite sane' and she had never exhibited 'any suicidal tendencies'. It was assumed that Elizabeth must have decided to visit her daughter Mary, who was working in Maidenhead, and that in crossing the railway line, she was knocked down and killed. The jury recorded a verdict of accidental death and the coroner noted that there had been other fatalities in the same place, and that he had already alerted the town council and the railway company to the need for a bridge there. Whether Elizabeth intended to kill herself, we will never know, but a stigma was attached to suicide that perhaps made a verdict of accidental death more likely. The family was described in the newspaper report of the inquest as 'well-known and held in much respect in Maidenhead and the neighbourhood of the Thicket'.[17]

Joseph and the three remaining children had to make their own lives without her. By 1911, George and John had moved out, and Joseph, still living on the grounds of Woolley Hall, shared his home with Mary, who kept house. After retirement, the widowed Joseph moved to 41, Spencers Road, a two-bedroomed house in Maidenhead. He remained in the town for the rest of his life, dying in 1944 at the age of 91.

The children had varying fortunes.

George, the son whom Elizabeth tried to kill, married Agnes in 1919, and they moved to Canada where they had four children. George lived until 1966, dying in Winnipeg. His descendants still live in Canada. Mary remained in Maidenhead, marrying William Roberts in 1914. They lived with Joseph at 41, Spencers Road: it must have been a little cramped. She died in 1932, aged only 46. The fate of John Francis, a baby when Elizabeth was taken to Broadmoor, was even sadder. He died in the First World War aged 25. A member of the Royal Garrison Artillery, he was killed in in the Punjab, and buried in Rawalpindi War Cemetery.

There was also Mary Ann, of course. Elizabeth's half-sister lived a long life after her marriage to William Gibney. In 1901, they had six children living at home (Sarah, George, Thomas, William, Mary and Helena), ranging in age from 13 to baby Helena.

In 1908, Mary Ann's husband William died, leaving her a relatively young widow, and Mary Ann took work as a dressmaker. Most of her children did well for themselves, and lived long lives, but William, like so many other young men, was killed in the Battle of the Somme, aged only 21. Mary Ann herself died in 1933, aged 76.

Chapter 5

Blanche Bastable

Eliza Blanche Bastable, known to her family as Blanche, was the youngest person in this book to be admitted to Broadmoor. When she committed her crime, she was a single woman living at home with her family. Unlike others whose stories we recount here, her life was not blighted by poverty. Nonetheless, something happened to her mental state that led her to carry out a particularly shocking murder.

Blanche was born in the village of East Orchard in Dorset, in 1852 to George, a dairy farmer, and Elizabeth, both 30 at the time of her birth. Elizabeth Cole, a grocer's daughter, had married George in January 1849 at the parish church of Milford in Hampshire, Elizabeth's home town. Before marriage, Elizabeth worked as a dressmaker, while George, the eldest of ten siblings, had already inherited the medium-sized family farm from his father John, who had died in 1846. (In the 1861 census, George is described as farming 32 acres, and in the 1881 census 52½ acres. Either one of those is a mistake or George took on more land in that time.) Blanche was their second child. Their first, Mary Jane, had been born in December 1850.

Living with them at Winchell's Farm were George's widowed mother Mary, his brother John, 23, and sister Eliza, 14.

Dorset at the time was a particularly poor county. Agricultural labourers were badly paid, earning as little as six shillings a week. In contrast, as a yeoman farmer, George Bastable was comparatively well-off. In the small society in which they lived, the Bastables ranked relatively high on the social scale. Owning and running a family farm was hard work, but they owned the seven-roomed farmhouse and the land that went with it. They would not have wanted for food. They were also fortunate to have a garden, something that was a rarity for town-dwellers.

East Orchard was a farming village, with a population of just over 200: Winchell's was one of ten farms. It was separated by a brook, Orchard Water, from the neighbouring village of West Orchard. Although small, East Orchard possessed a church, St Thomas's, which dated from Norman times, and, from 1867, a village primary school. This was one of a number of schools run by an organization attached to the Church of England, which had been founded with the aim of providing a free education to poorer children. Children learnt to read and write, and there was a heavy emphasis on religious instruction. These schools (known as 'National' schools) were the precursor to the system of state schools.

Growing up in East Orchard, Blanche's life must have been very different from that of most of the other women featured in this book. Rather than living in a cramped space in a smoky, dirty city, she would have lived much of her life outdoors. No doubt the children would have helped their mother from a young age with household tasks and jobs such as milking the cows. Social contact, however, would have been limited to a handful of local families. A taste of town life, or a visit to the shops, would have required a trip either to Sturminster Newton four miles away, or Shaftesbury, the same distance in the other direction. If the names seem familiar, that is because East Orchard was in the heart of what we now call Hardy country. Both towns had existed for approximately 1,000 years: Sturminster Newton, where Hardy and his new wife lived between 1876 and 1878, is first recorded in 968, while Shaftesbury had been founded by King Alfred 100 years earlier.

Shaftesbury has existed under a variety of different names, one of which, Shaston, is the name by which Hardy refers to it in his novels. It features particularly heavily in *Jude the Obscure* as the place where Phillotson, Sue Bridehead's husband, runs a school. Jude and Sue elope from Shaston together. It also gets a brief mention in *Tess of the d'Urbervilles* – Jack Durbeyfield visits his doctor in Shaston. Shaftesbury was most famous for the abbey, built by Alfred the Great, and destroyed by Henry VIII during the Reformation. According to Hardy's account in *Jude the Obscure*, the bones of King Edward the Martyr, murdered in 978, had made the town a draw for pilgrims from all over Europe, but after the destruction of the abbey the 'whole place collapsed in general ruin: the Martyr's bones met with the fate of the sacred pile that held them, and not a stone is now left to tell where they lie'.[1]

Its historic towns apart, Dorset's economy was largely based on agriculture, and in the middle of the century was home to 2,500 farms.[2] Most of those were focused on dairy farming: the county's butter was apparently particularly highly rated.[3] One peculiarity of the way dairy farmers (and hence the Bastables) worked in the county was that the farmer 'did not manage his own herd but instead hired the animals out to a specialist dairyman at a fixed price per animal, the exact figure varying in accordance with the quality of the land and the produce of the beast'.[4]

In the nineteenth century, however, there was almost nowhere untouched by the industrial revolution. This seemingly tranquil rural world into which Blanche was born was rapidly changing. The advent of the trains had given a boost to dairy farmers, enabling them to transport fresh milk to London and other cities. At the same time, yeomen farmers like the Bastables were in decline, to be replaced by large capitalist farms. The county's villages were also experiencing depopulation, as many tradesmen and their families moved to the cities. In *Tess of the d'Urbevilles*, set in the 1870s, Hardy mourns the loss of people who had given the county's towns and villages a particular character:

> The village had formerly contained, side by side with the agricultural labourers, an interesting and better-informed class, ranking distinctly above the former — the class

> to which Tess's father and mother had belonged — and including the carpenter, the smith, the shoemaker, the huckster, together with nondescript workers other than farm-labourers; a set of people who owed a certain stability of aim and conduct to the fact of their being life-holders like Tess's father, or copy-holders, or occasionally, small freeholders. But as the long holdings fell in they were seldom again let to similar tenants, and were mostly pulled down, if not absolutely required by the farmer for his hands. Cottagers who were not directly employed on the land were looked on with disfavour, and the banishment of some starved the trade of others, who were thus obliged to follow.[5]

Mary Jane and Blanche were joined over the next thirteen years by six more siblings: Juliana, Eliza Ann, Georgina, Emma, John and George William. They were born at a time when it was becoming normal for children, including girls, to receive a formal education. Rather than attend the village's National school, the three girls were sent to very small private boarding schools: Mary Jane to one in Stour Provost, three miles away, which was run by Elizabeth Wilkins, the wife of a labourer, and Blanche and Juliana to one in Shaftesbury run by a widow named Matilda Isham. (Matilda no doubt had her own story: her late husband, Justinian, with whom she had four children, was an attorney's writing clerk who had been born in the West Indies. Probably the school was a way of making ends meet after his death when he was still in his early 40s.) If it seems curious that George and Elizabeth would send their daughters away to board when there was a free school a short walk away, then the answer might lie in social class. The nineteenth-century Dorset writer Richard Jeffries observed that once labourers' children began attending school, they acquired the taint of 'pauperism', so many farmers chose to send their children to fee-paying schools.[6] Why the 10-year-old Mary Jane went to a different school from Blanche and Julianna is an unsolved mystery.

Remarkably, the Bastables' eight children all survived infancy – perhaps a testament to the advantages of living in the countryside rather than the overcrowded towns and cities. No doubt, living on a dairy farm, they would have been well fed too. In December 1870, however, tragedy struck when Mary Jane died of tuberculosis (or haemoptysis phthisis as it was recorded on the death certificate) at the age of 20. By 1871, John, who was now 13, had been sent to a boarding school called Stourpaine House, just a few miles away. Juliana was employed as a dairy maid, probably for her father, while Blanche, now 19, worked as a teacher to the younger children, Georgina, Emma and George.

Within a few years, however, Blanche was showing signs of mental illness. One wonders if the loss of Mary Jane, so close in age, had anything to do with it, though none of the court reports or asylum records mention this as a possibility. Like so many other women who ended up in Broadmoor, her illness took the form of religious mania. In August 1875, the family decided to put her in Brislington House, near Bristol, a private institution and one of the first purpose-built mental asylums in Britain. Opened in 1804, it was one of the first asylums to use the gentler 'moral' therapies that were eventually to become widely accepted in asylums throughout the country. Like the Tukes who had founded the pioneering York Retreat, Dr Edward Long Fox who founded Brislington House was a Quaker who believed in the importance of nature and the consolation of being in a domestic environment. Patients were encouraged to take part in gentle leisure activities such as exercise, gardening and music. The asylum had the appearance of a grand, three-storey country house, set in 300 acres (120 hectares) of beautiful gardens, pleasure grounds and farmland.

After she returned home in June 1876, a farm labourer called William Lodge was hired to look after her, as a precaution. William found his charge fairly easy to manage, and didn't think she was likely to cause anyone any harm. On 26 September 1877, there was a family outing to Shroton Fair, at which Blanche, her mother and two of her sisters were accompanied by William. As lovers of Hardy will know, fairs were an important part of rural life: most memorably, *The Mayor of Casterbridge* opens with Michael Henchard selling his wife Susan at a fair in the fictional town of Weydon-Priors.

Shroton Fair was a huge, and immensely popular, annual event that lasted three days. It had been going since the thirteenth century and was famous for its horse, sheep and cheese sales as well as the opportunity to hire labourers and domestic servants. No doubt for the Bastables and other local families, it would have been one of the highlights of the calendar. We know that Thomas Hardy himself, who was then living in Sturminster Newton and writing *The Return of the Native*, visited Shroton Fair on 25 September 1877, the day before the Bastables' visit. This is what he wrote about the experience in his diary:

> Went to Shroton Fair. In a twopenny show saw a woman beheaded. In another a man whose hair grew on one side of his face. Coming back across Hambledon Hill (where the Club-Men assembled, *temp.* Cromwell)[7] a fog came on. I nearly got lost in the dark inside the earthworks, the old hump-backed man I had parted from on the other side of the hill, who was going somewhere else before coming across the earthworks in my direction, being at the bottom as soon as I. A man might go round and round all night in such a place.[8]

The local paper doesn't carry an account of the 1877 Shroton Fair: the previous year it had reported that there were a 'large number of pleasure seekers' but that little business was done, except by the 'owners of shows, steam round-abouts, shooting galleries &c'.[9] In 1877, the Bastables, like Hardy, were among the pleasure seekers. We don't know if they saw the woman being beheaded or the hairy man, but Blanche expressed the desire to shoot at two of the rifle galleries. She shot twice at each, and did so very well.

Her condition deteriorated, however, and in late October, her father said, she became 'more depressed, and at times excited and morose'. The family began considering placing her in Fisherton House Asylum, another private asylum based just outside Salisbury, and took the advice of the local surgeon, Mr Curme, who had been visiting the house to attend one of Blanche's sisters. Elizabeth took the opportunity to tell him that the family did not feel safe in the house with Blanche around, and he recommended that she arrange to take her to Fisherton as soon as possible. Blanche herself was out, having gone to Hartgrove to be measured for boots, and Mr Curme expressed his view that she should not be out so late. Heeding his advice, Elizabeth made arrangements to travel to the asylum with her son John on Tuesday to meet Dr John Lush, the asylum's superintendent.

On Monday, 5 November 1877, Blanche spent most of the morning sewing. Mid-afternoon, William left her for a few minutes to help out with some farm work. Elizabeth, meanwhile, had been baking. The design of the house was such that, instead of a front door and a back door, it had two doors on the same side, seven yards apart, both opening out into the garden, which faced the road. Not knowing where Blanche was, Elizabeth walked through one of the two front doors into the garden to look for her. Blanche, still indoors, walked over to a rack where her uncle John, a cowman employed by a local landowner called Colonel Lloyd-Lindsay, kept a single-barrelled gun. John had loaded the gun at about 1 pm, and taken it outside with the intention of killing some rooks. He did not fire it, however, but brought it back in ten minutes and placed it in its usual position above the fireplace.

Blanche picked up the gun, walked into the garden through a second door, and found her mother, who was standing with her back toward her. From a distance of about seven yards, she aimed it at her mother's head and fired. Her mother fell and died instantly, not even

The Hospital of Bethlem (Bedlam), St. George's Fields, Lambeth: the female workroom. A wood engraving probably by F. Vizetelly after F. Palmer, 1860. (Wellcome Collection. Attribution 4.0 International (CC BY 4.0))

Bethlem Hospital, London: the incurables being inspected by a member of the medical staff, with the patients represented by political figures. A drawing by Thomas Rowlandson, 1789. (Wellcome Collection. Attribution 4.0 International (CC BY 4.0))

Façade and gardens of Brislington House, one of the first purpose-built asylums for the insane. An engraving after S. C. Jones, c.1865. (Wellcome Library, London. Reproduced under Creative Commons Attribution only licence (CC BY 4.0))

York Retreat, exterior. (Attribution 4.0 International (CC BY 4.0))

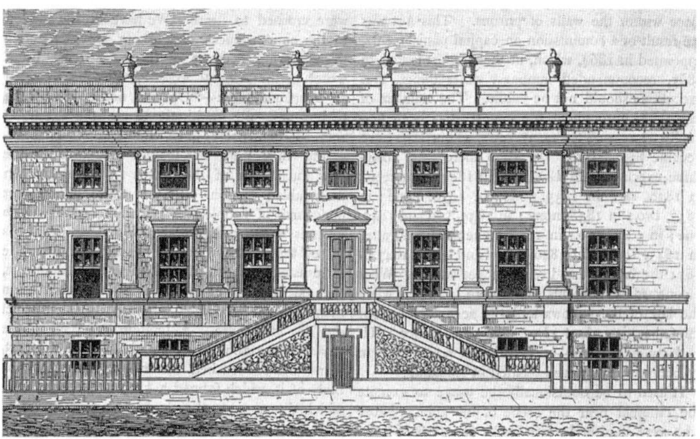

Exterior of the Surgeons' Hall at the Old Bailey, London, 1775. (Wellcome Collection. Attribution 4.0 International (CC BY 4.0))

Colney Hatch Lunatic Asylum, Southgate, Middlesex: panoramic view.

Patients dancing at Colney Hatch Lunatic Asylum, published in *The Illustrated London News*. (Wellcome Collection. Attribution 4.0 International (CC BY 4.0))

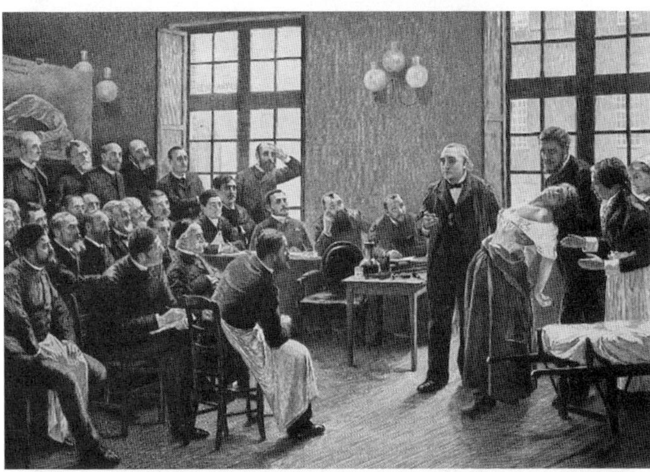

The French psychiatrist Jean-Martin Charcot demonstrating hysteria in a hypnotized patient to an audience of medical students at the Salpêtrière. Etching by A. Lurat, 1888, after P. A. A. Brouillet, 1887. (Attribution 4.0 International (CC BY 4.0))

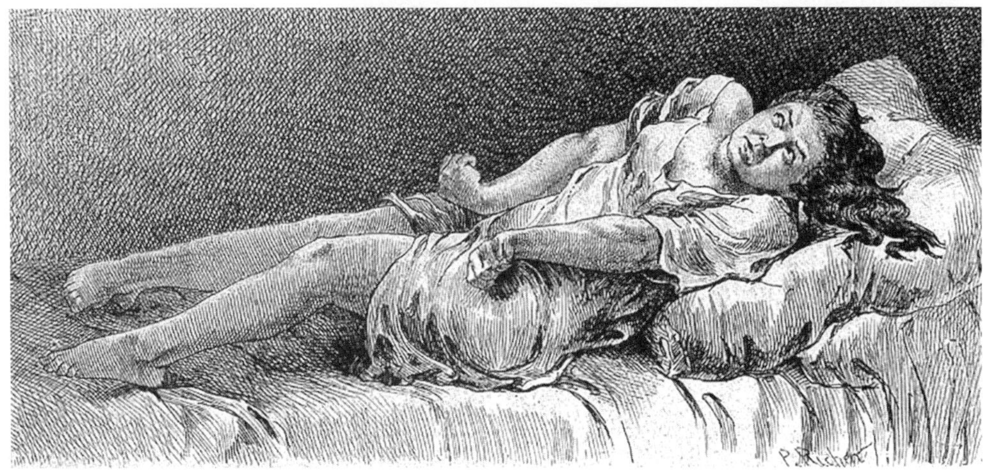

A woman in the grip of a hysterical fit. From a series of photographic studies by Paul Richer, 1881, with an introduction by Charcot. (Reproduced by permission of the Wellcome Library, London)

Postcard showing main entrance to Broadmoor c. 1910.

Postcard showing Broadmoor from the outside c. 1910.

Above: View of Broadmoor in the Berkshire countryside published in *The Illustrated London News*, 1867. (Permission of Reading Libraries)

Right: Postcard of the female entrance to Broadmoor c. 1910.

Another view of the entrance to the women's quarters, c. 1910.

An external shot of Broadmoor's female quarters, c. 1910

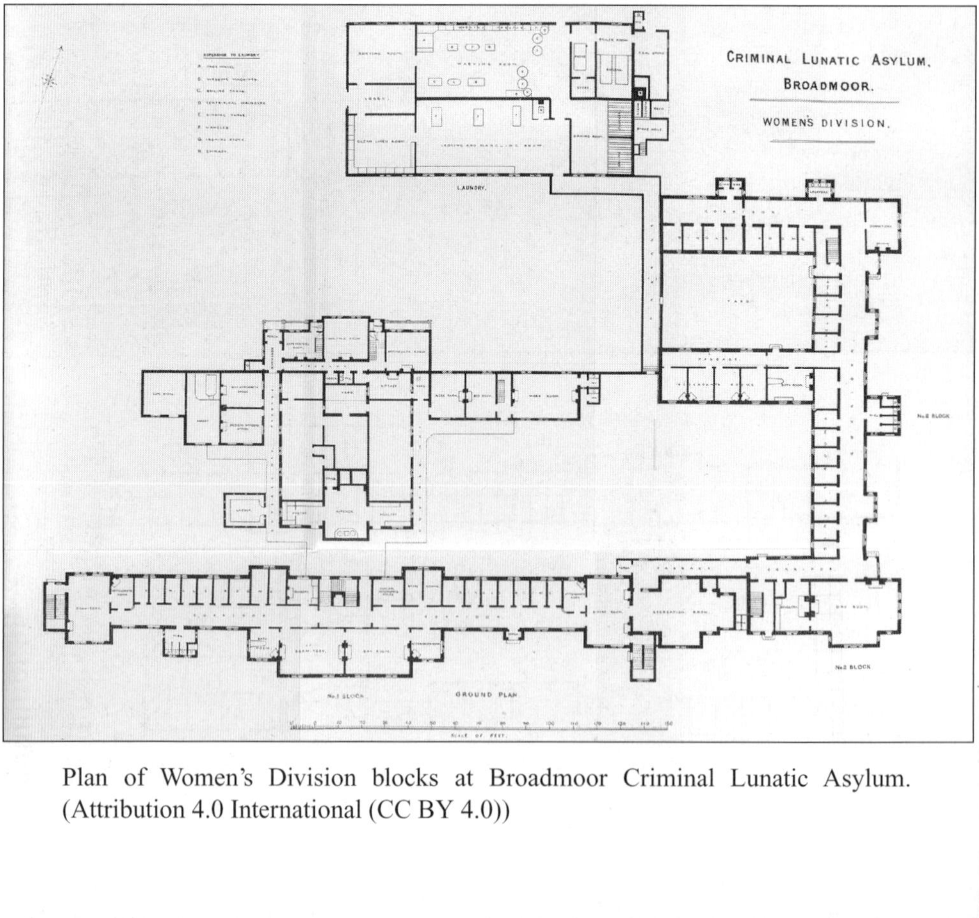

CRIMINAL LUNATIC ASYLUM,
BROADMOOR.
WOMEN'S DIVISION.

LAUNDRY.

GROUND PLAN

SCALE OF FEET.

Plan of Women's Division blocks at Broadmoor Criminal Lunatic Asylum. (Attribution 4.0 International (CC BY 4.0))

Right: Broadmoor women's dormitory, published in *The Illustrated London News*, 1867. (Permission of Reading Libraries)

Below: Women at Broadmoor dancing as the asylum band plays, published in *The Illustrated London News*, 1867. (Permission of Reading Libraries)

The day room reserved for male patients at Broadmoor, published in *The Illustrated London News*, 1867. (Photo by HultonArchive/ Getty Images)

Broadmoor's female staff c. 1900, including the sisters Ellen Tyman (top left) and Gertrude Tyman (seated, second from right). The woman in the centre is probably Elizabeth Morgan, the chief female attendant, who worked at Broadmoor for over thirty years.

Patients and staff on the terrace, 1908, looking east across one of the lower terraces, with the edge of Block 2 in the background. (From Hargrave L. Adam's book, *The Story of Crime*.)

letting out a scream. Hearing the gunshot, her father rushed from the farmyard to the garden, along with several neighbours.

Blanche's sister Emma was in her mother's bedroom when she heard the gunshot. She looked out of the window and saw her mother lying on the ground. Emma shouted to her father: 'Mamma is dead! Mamma is dead!'

As Emma went down the stairs, she met Blanche on the way up. Blanche, Emma testified, 'passed me without saying a word, and went on to her bedroom'. About half an hour later, Emma found the gun upright against the wall, near the bottom of the stairs.

George testified that he had last seen his wife at about 4.30, sitting in the kitchen next to the fire. He left to drive the cows into the yard for milking, and having done so, heard the report of a gun. He told the inquest what happened next:

> I looked round and saw smoke near the kitchen door at which my daughter Blanche was standing. I did not notice that she had anything in her hand, but she was standing still looking in the direction where I afterwards found my wife. I then heard a scream, and, on asking my daughter Emma what was the matter, she said, 'Mamma is dead.' I then saw my wife lying on the ground upon her face in the garden walk close to the front door. I went to her and found that she was dead, with blood flowing from her mouth, and a wound in the back of the head. I then enquired for Blanche who had left the place I had seen her standing at. My wife was 55 years of age last birthday. I went to look for my daughter Blanche, whom I suspected of having fired off the gun by which my wife was killed. There was no one else near.[10]

William, having been called by George, went into the garden and saw the body. He then returned to the house, where he saw Blanche coming down the stairs. He took hold of her and they walked out into the garden together. As they passed the body, Blanche said: 'Let me lift her up; she is not dead; she only sleepeth; she will rise again.' She was, said William, in the habit of quoting scripture (the line is from the Gospel of Luke). William asked her why she had killed her mother, and Blanche replied: 'It was God's will that I should do it.' She kept calling out of the window, 'Mamma, mamma, do answer me,' William said, adding that Blanche claimed that the gun had been put there on purpose to tempt her, and that it had been tempting her a long time.

In the evening, George's brother John – the owner of the gun – arrived and stayed with the family. The local surgeon, Mr Curme, arrived at about 7 pm, and examined Elizabeth's body, which had been laid out on the sofa. He provided the inquest with a graphic account of her head injuries and concluded that death had been instantaneous. He went upstairs to see Blanche, and asked her why she had killed her mother. After a moment's hesitation, she replied very calmly: 'Well, the law must be fulfilled, all the wicked shall be abolished off the earth.' She then went on: 'She will live again in Jesus.'

Later in the evening, the superintendent of police, John Pitfield, arrived and saw Elizabeth's body on the sofa with a large wound in her head exposing her brain. He went into the garden where he said he found the gun in a flowerbed. (This contradicts Emma's evidence, which was that Blanche had brought the gun indoors.) He went indoors and told Blanche that he was taking her into custody, to which Blanche replied, 'Oh.' She then added: 'You are evil in my eyes, and so are you, William.'

At the inquest, the verdict of the jury was murder, and Blanche was arrested. Four days after her mother's death, she was taken to the town hall in Shaftesbury and charged with the wilful murder of Elizabeth Bastable. She was dressed in a 'grey Lindsey dress, seal skin jacket, and straw hat'. (Linsey is a plain fabric made with linen warp and woollen weft threads.) In her pocket, she carried a bible. According to the newspaper report, Blanche paid no attention to the proceedings except when she recognized a name, at which point she would 'look with a wild stare towards the person named'. It added: 'The poor girl did not seem, in the slightest degree, to feel the awful nature of the charge against her.' In reply to the chairman of the bench, she said: 'I have nothing to say.' Blanche was then formally committed to trial for wilful murder at Dorset Assizes. In the meantime, she was remanded to the county prison in Dorchester.

In fact, Blanche was not to stand trial. The secretary of state decided she was insane and ordered her removal to Charminster Lunatic Asylum, one of two county asylums in Dorset. (The other was in Forston.) It must have been a difficult place for a young woman to stay. The report from the medical superintendent, Gustavus Symes, for 1877 grumbled that the two asylums were 'filling with old, demented, paralyzed, and worn-out cases' rather than people who were truly mentally ill. He complained too that a source of the increase in patients was the 'very irregular fast, intemperate way in which they live; many, too, smoke immoderately, a habit few can indulge in without evil effects showing themselves sooner or later'.[11] Visiting in 1878, the commissioners in lunacy reported that the two asylums were nearly full, but they were largely positive, saying that the 'wards are far more cheerful than they were, by the introduction of color [sic], and some ordinary comforts' and that the 'rule of the Superintendent is wise and kindly'.[12]

She was only there for a few months, however, before being removed, in April 1878, to Broadmoor. Her admission record stated that her current attack of mental illness had lasted one and a half to two years, but that she had had previous attacks. The cause of her insanity was unknown, but her chief delusion was that she 'believes herself called on by God to destroy some person or persons'. Her bodily health was described as 'fair', but she had recently had a bout of pneumonia. Her education was described as 'very fair indeed'.

Blanche was one of sixteen women to be admitted to Broadmoor in 1878. Of those sixteen women, nine had committed murder, while five were convict patients, who had been serving prison sentences. That year the asylum had 483 patients: 374 men, and 109 women. It was a good year for Broadmoor, with only ten deaths, but no suicides, no infectious diseases and no serious accidents.[13]

Schedule A, the form filled in by the head of Dorset Asylum when she was admitted to Broadmoor, mentions that Blanche had had pneumonia three months earlier. The cause of her insanity is given as 'congenital'. William Orange's own notes on admission describe Blanche as 'the subject of religious mania & highly erotic & excitable'. He writes of her appearance that she 'has a pleasing expression of face which is altered from time to time by a fixed & staring condition of the eyes & by a compression of the lips'. Of her temperament, he writes:

> Incoherent, wild & flighty in her conversation. Irritable, & has numerous delusions respecting her personality. States that she has read the Bible much & that she was called upon by what it told her to kill her mother, & that she would do the same to others if called upon by God. Health tolerably good.

Shortly after arriving, she sent a letter to one of her sisters. Whatever was in it caused the sister some uneasiness. The sister (we don't know which one because the signature is missing) then replied with an accompanying letter to Orange, reading:

> I received a letter from her several weeks ago, but dreaded answering it, as it makes me feel so ill, & don't know how

> to write to her, should feel very grateful to you if you would kindly write sometimes to let us know how she is.

Orange sent a reply to George:

> I write to say that I have given her sister's letter to your daughter. I will with pleasure answer your inquiries with respect to your daughter whenever you may wish to write to ask about her. There has not at present been much alteration in her condition since she was admitted.

In September that year, Blanche's condition remained unchanged. According to Orange, she had 'chronic mania with exacerbations'. Describing her behaviour, he wrote:

> Wilful & sometimes almost violent, catching hold of the attendants when not allowed to do exactly as she wishes. At times will not get out of bed for some hours. Restless, hysterical & crying. Now & again cheerful & pleasant. Reads the bible when she reads anything. Has written to her friends once or twice, on one occasion asking about her mother as if she were alive.

Sadly, Blanche's stay in Broadmoor was to be a short one. In an undated written note (but probably from 1879) Orange mentions her consumption, and says that 'her mind continues to be much deranged.' In April 1879, he wrote of her: 'Health generally not good. Cough & defective circulation. Mentally restless & full of whims & delusions which at times render her unsafe among the others. Requires careful watching.'

A note dated 26 August 1879 records that Blanche is 'seriously ill suffering from consumption' and 'spitting blood' but that she is 'supplied with everything her condition requires.'

Things got worse. In September Blanche's case notes read:

> Health giving way – has become very phthisical [consumptive] & has had several attacks of haemoptysis [coughing up blood], some of them very profuse. Gets thinner. Will not take medicine regularly. Has been ordered cod liver oil & tonics. Appetite capricious. Much coughing. Dulness [*sic*] on percussion both lungs, especially left. Crepitation [crackling sound in the lungs] & moist sounds. Mentally much deranged.

By the end of the year, there was no hope. On 20 December Orange wrote: 'In last stage of consumption. Loud moist sounds. Large cavities. Hectic, with occasional diarrhoea.'

A note dated 9 January 1880 says that Blanche's father should be informed that Blanche is in a 'very precarious condition' but that she is in the sick ward and 'supplied with everything that is necessary for her.'

On 14 January 1880, her notes record: 'Has gradually (although with both lungs diseased throughout) lost ground & died this morning at 7.30, of pulmonary consumption.'

The same day Orange wrote the following rather terse note to George:

> I beg to inform you that your daughter, Eliza Blanche Bastable, died this day. … Her funeral is fixed to take place on Monday, the 19th inst at 1/4 past 2 of clock, unless you would prefer to remove her body for burial, in which case please reply by return of post.

Blanche was one of twenty patients to die that year at Broadmoor – an unusually high number, which Orange attributed partly to the 'severe winter of 1879–80'.[14] The inquest confirmed that she died of pulmonary consumption – what we now know as tuberculosis.[15]

Her father did not remove her body for burial and we don't even know whether the family attended the funeral. After the service, Blanche, only 27 years of age, was buried at St John's Church in Crowthorne. This wasn't unusual for Broadmoor patients, especially the poorer ones, but it meant, as Jade Shepherd has pointed out, that graves remained 'empty' and 'unadorned', in contrast to most Victorian graves, which were typically used as a means of commemoration, through headstones, gifts of flowers and frequent visits.[16]

Life, of course, went on without her. Tragedy struck again in 1883 when Georgina died aged 27, the same age as Blanche. She too had pulmonary tuberculosis, which led to a perforated ulceration of the bowel. Georgina was buried in St Thomas's churchyard, alongside her mother Elizabeth, and her sister Mary Jane. They were later joined by their father George, who died in 1897 at the age of 77. The farm was passed down to the two brothers, John and George. By 1901, it was just the two of them – John now 41, George, 35 – living at Winchell's, along with a housekeeper. Ten years later, the two men remained, still unmarried, but with a different housekeeper. Shortly afterwards, they sold the farm that had been in the family for generations and went their separate ways. George married a woman named Dorothea, and moved to Mill Farm, a few miles away. They had a son and daughter together, and George remained at the farm until his death in 1943. John, meanwhile, took over Peakes Farm, just a few miles away in Sedgehill, and died in 1918.

Juliana married a local East Orchard man, Jordan Richard Shute, who ran Trapdoor Farm. Like Blanche, she was to spend some time in Dorset County Asylum, before dying in 1915 at the age of 61. Her only son, George, predeceased her. Eliza Ann died, unmarried, in 1901.

Emma, the youngest daughter, married a farmer named Thomas Lear in 1886, and they had twelve children, two of whom died in infancy. She died in 1933.

There is a strange coda to this sad story. In 1948, Winchell's Farm was occupied by Frederick and Eva Shute (surely related to Juliana's husband Jordan, though I haven't been able to establish a connection) and their 12-year-old son George. George suffered very severely from epilepsy, and his seizures were often prefaced by bouts of bad temper. One morning, at the end of November, he became angry that his breakfast wasn't quite to his liking, found his father's shotgun, loaded it and, using a curtain rod to pull the trigger, shot himself in the chest. He died instantly.[17]

Chapter 6

Rebecca Loveridge

Rebecca Shewring (sometimes spelt Shurin) was born on 8 October 1845 in Westminster, London, to Ann and James. They lived on a street named Perkin's Rents, sited in a grim locality that Dickens referred to as 'The Devil's Acre'. According to the journalist Vic Keegan, no other area in London was 'quite as abominable as this territory a few hundred yards away from the sublimity of Westminster Abbey and the Houses of Parliament'. Keegan adds that it was its nearness to Westminster Abbey that caused so many of its problems. Apparently, there was a large area of land outside the abbey that, thanks to a decree of Edward the Confessor, had become a sanctuary where criminals were safe from the law: 'It thus became a magnet for disreputables and the tradition lingered long after the abolition of sanctuary.' In Dickens's own magazine, *Household Words*, he describes the area, with his usual flourish, as 'begirt by scenes of indescribable infamy and pollution; the blackest tide of moral turpitude that flows in the capital rolls its filthy wavelets up to the very walls of Westminster Abbey.'[1] Each house in Perkin's Rents was multi-occupancy: the Shewrings probably shared number 11 with numerous other tenants. The street was also home to a pub known as the Old Tun, which was regarded as a school for pickpockets, and may even have served as the inspiration for Oliver Twist.

Given the rarity of the name Shewring, James has left little trace in the historical record. He seems to have been born in the Marylebone workhouse in 1811, the illegitimate child of Elizabeth Shewring and John Collins, who may have married the following year. We know nothing of Ann, except that her maiden name was Pritchard.

We do know that James worked as a shoemaker and that he was also, unfortunately, a drunkard who died by suicide. Rebecca never learnt to read and write.

Given her unpromising start in life, we shouldn't be surprised that as a teenager, she took to travelling and selling goods. This was a relatively common occupation in the nineteenth century for young, working-class women with limited options. It was possible to travel the country, going from town to town and selling goods either on the street or at a market. In the years 1849–51 Henry Mayhew estimated that there were between 30,000 and 40,000 people who made their income from street-selling.[2] The goods they sold included fruit, vegetables, coffee and second-hand clothing. Although some of these hawkers were licensed, a large minority were unlicensed sellers working illegally.

It was a financially precarious occupation. A report into women's work at the end of the nineteenth century found that hawking brought in very little money. One widow with five children, for example, sold her goods in the street from 10 to 1 every day. Each afternoon, she would buy second-hand items, which she would then mend and clean in preparation for selling them the following morning. Most days, however, she didn't earn anything at all. Another woman, a mother of seven, spent her entire life as a fish hawker. Some weeks the family would make £1, but others they would lose £1. Another woman said her husband had been made redundant from his steady job and, 'there being no further work available, had set up a barrow which she helped to run'.[3]

Mayhew also noted that a number of married couples went hawking together and that the wives were often beaten by their husbands. Many couples would introduce their children to the profession, with infants as young as seven sometimes going out on the street to sell their wares. For young single women working alone, of course, the job also brought the risk of sexual predation.

Rebecca's speciality seems to have been 'fancy' articles and 'Birmingham ware' (probably jewellery and silverware). Her work as a hawker took her to Newport in South Wales. While there, she met a fellow hawker, George Loveridge. George, three years older, had been born in the small village of Taynton in Gloucestershire. He operated at least some of the time without a licence – in 1861, he was sentenced to seven days' hard labour for hawking without a licence in Tredegar and, what is more, having the words 'licensed hawker' on his basket in an attempt to deceive the public.[4]

In 1865, when Rebecca was only 18 and George 21, the pair were married in Newport. For some time after that, they appear to have continued working as hawkers, travelling the country together. Their first child, also named Rebecca, was born in 1866 in Plymouth. It's possible they took the baby with them on their travels, at least for a while. Their second baby, Sarah Ann, was born in 1868, but died a few months later. By the time George was born in 1870, the family had settled in Newton Abbott, a market town in Devon. George senior was still travelling, however: at the time of the 1871 census, he was staying without wife or children in a hotel in the Isle of Man, and giving his job as 'commercial traveller'. Seven years later, he was operating legally as a licensed pedlar. In 1879, the family moved from the house they had rented for seven years, at a cost of £30 a year, to Oakford Farm in nearby Kingsteignton, a village with a population of about 1,600 people.[5] The farmhouse had five rooms: small by today's standards, but more comfortable, perhaps, than what the family had previously been used to.

George's new life as a farmer included not only raising pigs and dairy cattle, but horse-dealing, which involved attending fairs around the county where he bought and sold horses – a job that would have kept him busy. Even after the arrival of the railways, horses were still an important form of transport: one estimate is that in 1888, there were about half a million carts and vans in Britain, all pulled by horses.[6] They were also, of course, widely used in farming. Horse-dealing was one of those occupations fraught with the potential for dishonesty, and George's name turns up a few times, mostly as a witness, in newspaper stories of disputes over horse sales. Rebecca, it seems, continued to work, travelling around the local area during the day to sell her wares – though George insisted she also work feeding and bedding the horses. At her trial, the judge was to describe her life as 'almost that of a slave'.

She was also giving birth every two years. John was born in 1872, followed by Rose in 1874, Henry in 1876, Frederick in 1878, Florence in 1881 and then Jessie in 1883. The children all attended school. Kingsteignton had two: one run by the Church of England, the other a non-denominational school. The Loveridge children probably attended the former.

The marriage was far from a happy one. George was a drunk with a violent temper, and he subjected Rebecca to frequent beatings. This was not uncommon at the time. In 1878, Frances Power Cobbe wrote that 'the men of the lower class … are proverbial for their unparalleled brutality'.[7] Cobbe despaired of the fact that wealthier men did nothing to stop the violence working-class men inflicted on their wives. There was no easy avenue of escape: divorce was extremely expensive, and women were often denied contact with their children. There was little recourse in law either – the 1853 Criminal Procedure Act had made it possible to prosecute men for domestic violence if it was sufficiently extreme, but sending the main breadwinner to prison for six months would throw his wife and children into poverty.[8] In any case, as Jenna Dodenhoff has written, 'physical violence was generally accepted and expected among the working class'. It was, she adds, considered 'improper for neighbors to intervene in an altercation between husband and wife, which was regarded as a natural part of marriage.'[9]

Rebecca also worried about her elder children: the two boys, George and John, refused to go and work in the stables, preferring to play instead. She was forced to do their work for them, as well as her own housework. Her eldest daughter, Rebecca, now 18, was often cheeky to her.

After Jessie's birth, Rebecca reached the stage where she couldn't take any more. On Friday, 11 January 1884, she was once more subjected to George's temper. At about 9.45 in the morning, the local butcher, William Ward (named as Richard Ward in one report), arrived at their farm to kill one of the pigs, at George's request. George asked Rebecca: 'Bec, is the water ready to scald the pig with?' Rebecca answered, 'No, I haven't had time to do it,' to which George's response, according to Ward's evidence at the inquest, was, 'You lazy wretch; what have you been about?' accompanied by a kick. (At the magistrates' hearing, 'wretch' became 'bitch', which feels more plausible.) George then put the horse in its harness and Ward helped him to put it in the trap (usually Rebecca's work) to go to Teignmouth. Ward told Rebecca he was going to Newton station and would call on his return at about 12.30 and kill the pig then if Rebecca could get the water hot in that time.

When Ward returned, Rebecca was waiting for him. Ten minutes later, George returned and Rebecca helped take the horse out of the trap and then, once it was in the stable, gave it a bran mash. On hearing that she'd done this, George asked her why she'd done it ('You bitch – what did you get that for?') and slapped her so hard that the imprint of his hand remained on her face. The entire time Ward was there, Rebecca cried and, referring to the recent suicide of a woman named Mrs Pinsent, said that it would be no different if she 'served herself the same way' as everyone treated her so badly.

At about seven in the evening, George returned home. Rebecca then left with the baby, determined to kill both herself and Jessie. She walked with the 11-month-old to the end of Kingsteignton's Homer Lane, where there was a disused claypit filled with water, thirty-five feet deep at its deepest point. She threw Jessie into the water, and then jumped in herself. Seemingly having second thoughts, she pulled Jessie out – before throwing her back in. Rebecca then tried to drown herself, but her clothes kept her afloat.

From there, Rebecca got out of the water and walked over to a van belonging to two acquaintances, Mr and Mrs Small. James Small was a horse-dealer, and his wife Ellen a hawker. En route, at about ten to nine, she was observed by a woman called Mary Ann Gibbs, who was returning home from Newton to Kingsteignton. The two women didn't speak to each other. According to Gibbs's testimony at the inquest, she was 'rambling', which she clarified to indicate that Rebecca was reeling as though intoxicated.

About half an hour later, she was observed by a plumber called Reginald Bulley, who passed so close by her that he could feel that her clothes were wet. She was not wearing a hat or bonnet, and didn't answer him when he wished her 'goodnight'. She was walking perfectly straight towards Newton, but 'wringing' her hands in an excited way.

Rebecca then arrived at the van of the Smalls. James Small heard something rattling against the glass of the door and saw a figure 'trembling and shaking to and fro, with her hands extended'. He then fell back exclaiming, 'Oh dear, there's a ghost.' Small, who seems to have been gifted with a sense of the dramatic, continues his testimony to the inquest: 'And believe me, sir, I trembled all over from hand to foot. I never was so frightened in all my life. Believe me sir, I did not know the woman.' Rebecca then apparently announced: 'I am Loveridge.'

Going outside, dressed in just his boots and trousers, Small saw that she was soaking wet. He told her, 'You're crazy drunk, you are.' Rebecca herself was in an 'excited state' and 'almost speechless'. Small called to some boys playing nearby, and told them that Rebecca was 'beastly drunk and wet'. He asked them to go with him to find George. In the meantime, Rebecca sat in the van with Ellen, rocking to and fro, and exclaiming, 'I have done it, I have done it.' In Ellen's view, 'I don't believe she knew what she was about.'

George, meanwhile, had gone out himself, and when he arrived home at about 9.30, he asked his 10-year-old daughter where her mother was. She replied that a woman, Miss Honey, had told her that she had seen Rebecca near the turnpike gate going towards Newton. George asked where the baby was, and she replied: 'Mother has got it.' He decided to go in search of Rebecca.

Small bumped into George on the road, and told him, 'George, your missus is drunk.' George asked if she had the baby with her, and Small told him that she didn't. They went back to the van, and George asked where the baby was. Rebecca said: 'I've drowned it! I've drowned it! I tried to drown myself too but I couldn't do it.' When he asked what made her do it, she replied, 'Because I was mad.'

As is so often the case, slightly different accounts of events were presented at the inquest, the magistrates' hearing and the full trial. One witness, Police Sergeant Nicholls, described seeing Rebecca and George standing in the marketplace at about 10 pm on the Friday night, surrounded by a crowd of people. The witness heard George ask: 'Rebecca, where have you put the baby?' to which she replied: 'I have drowned it at the big pond in Homer Lane.' Nicholls claimed not to have heard George ask Rebecca why she'd done it or Rebecca replying that she was mad.

Accompanied by his colleague Constable Salter and George, Nicholls then went to search for Jessie, and found her body floating on the pond, at a point where the water was only four or five inches deep. The body was near a broken rail which kept it from floating further down the stream. The baby, Nicholls later testified, was full grown and appeared well cared for. Although not wearing boots or stockings, she was otherwise fully dressed. In the lane, the police officers found Rebecca's soaking wet apron. Nicholls then put the body in a cab, and took it to the police station, where he also charged Rebecca with the murder of her child, to which she replied: 'Yes, I know; I did it.'

The local doctor, J. W. Lee, was called to the police station that evening and noted that the baby's body was covered in weed. Dr Lee also visited Rebecca in her cell and thought her incapable of giving a lucid account of what had happened. He warned Sergeant Nicholls that she was under the influence of 'suicidal mania'. (Later, he was to testify to magistrates that he had known Rebecca several years and believed that her suicidal tendencies were 'hereditary'.) He complained that the condition of the cell was totally unfit for a woman who had only that evening lost her sucking baby, but Nicholls told him that he had offered Rebecca the use of his office and fire, and she had refused it.

The following day, a Saturday, Dr Lee returned to assess the cause of death and concluded that the baby – 'a very fine child' – had drowned. That evening, the local undertaker, Robert Hammond, collected Jessie's body, placed it in a coffin and took it to the Loveridges' house.

Rebecca did not attend the inquest, held shortly afterwards, but a man named Mr Templer (probably from a local prisoners' association) attended on her behalf and testified that he had known her fourteen years and that he had never known her to be a drinking woman. He had seen her the night of Jessie's death and, although she was in a 'very excited' state, he was quite sure that she was not suffering from the effects of drink. He believed her to be a 'very steady and industrious woman' and that he 'never knew any harm against the woman in my life'. After hearing the evidence from Ward, Templer and the Smalls, the jury deliberated for twenty minutes and returned a verdict of 'wilful murder'.[10] Rebecca was then brought to the magistrates' court, where she was remanded for trial. The local newspaper reported that the court was crowded during the hearing, with 'much sympathy expressed for the prisoner'.[11] In the meantime, she was taken to Exeter gaol.

At her trial, held at the Devonshire Assizes only two weeks after the murder, even the prosecuting barrister, Mr Clarke, remarked that Rebecca was a 'most industrious woman and an excellent wife'. He added that she not only attended diligently to her household duties, but assisted her husband in the management of cattle, and had in all respects 'borne a most excellent character'. He went on to say that he was sorry he could not say the same of her husband, who had treated her very badly from time to time. It was up to Rebecca, he said, to show either that she did not drown her child, or that if she did, she was in such a state of mind that she couldn't be responsible for her actions. It's almost as if the prosecution was on Rebecca's side.

Rebecca's lawyer, Mr Pitt-Lewis, made an interesting if unlikely defence. He argued first that it was 'reasonable' to believe that Rebecca had gone outside and wandered about aimlessly before falling into the water with the child in her arms. (Given the evidence, this was hardly going to wash with the jury.) He went on to say that if the jury felt the charge of murder was supported, they would have to consider her state of mind: was she responsible? Was it likely, he went on, that an 'affectionate woman of sound mind' would deliberately seek to destroy her own life and that of her babe, and 'leave a lot of children motherless and exposed to the cruelty of a man at whose hands she had herself suffered such brutal treatment?' He asked for an acquittal.

In his summing-up, the judge remarked that the case was a 'sadder and more melancholy' one than he had ever come across in a court of justice. Rebecca's 'irreproachable conduct as a wife and mother' had met with a 'most shabby return' from her husband, whose conduct had been the direct cause of her being in the position in which she now stood. He said that the life Rebecca had lived was 'enough to unhinge the brain of any woman'. Although he said that the jury could hardly come to any conclusion other than that Rebecca had drowned her child, they would have to consider carefully the 'delicate' question of whether she was in a state of mind as to be responsible for her actions. The jury returned a written verdict: 'We find the prisoner guilty of causing the death of her child by drowning it, while attempting to take her own life, during temporary insanity.' They also condemned George's brutality towards her.

There is no sign in any of the newspaper reports of the inquest, magistrates' hearing or full trial of anyone showing anything other than sympathy towards Rebecca and her plight. Even though she had committed a terrible crime, and was perfectly well aware of what she was doing (which, according to the McNaughton rules, should have rendered her guilty), there was clearly a predisposition on the part of the judge and jury – and even, perhaps, the prosecution – to find her insane.

In court to hear Rebecca's case was a man named A. H. A. Hamilton, a magistrate and member of the Discharged Prisoners' Aid Society. This was a national organization that aimed to offer support to prisoners, particularly female prisoners, on their release. At the next meeting of the Devon and Exeter branch of the society, Hamilton brought up Rebecca's case, describing her as an industrious woman who was driven 'temporarily insane by brutality'. He proposed that as Rebecca was now 'perfectly sane', he thought it a cause that the society might take up to 'assist the poor woman to lead a happier and brighter life'.[12]

From the distance of the twenty-first century, it feels a little surprising that everyone accepted so readily the idea of 'temporary insanity'. Even if driven to the end of her tether, Rebecca clearly knew what she was doing, and very quickly after killing her baby apparently returned to sanity. There was enormous sympathy for a woman who had been subjected to years of cruelty, and a creditable desire to help her rather than punish her.

Rebecca arrived in Broadmoor from Exeter Prison in early February, one of 56 admissions that year. It was an eventful year at the asylum. Rebecca just missed a visit in January from the Empress Eugenie, Queen Victoria's daughter, which apparently provided a lively subject of conversation among patients for some time afterwards. This piece of drama was, however, trumped by an even more notable event: deputy superintendent David Nicolson was assaulted in September by a patient who, armed with two stones wrapped in a handkerchief, delivered a blow to the head, rendering Nicolson unable to work for six weeks.[13]

At Broadmoor, the superintendent, William Orange, found Rebecca showed every sign of being sane. He wrote that she gave 'a calm & rational account of herself & the circumstances connected with her offence'. She told him that she 'had "slaved" very hard to keep things going with her intemperate husband who was very exacting, thoughtless & unkind'. There were, he added, 'no prominent indications of insanity about her at present'.

Shortly after she arrived, Orange received a letter from the chairman of the visiting committee of Exeter Prison, forwarded to him from the Home Office. The visiting committee (a group of people appointed to oversee prisoners' conditions) seem to have called for her release, arguing that Rebecca was a respectable married woman driven into a 'state of temporary insanity by ill usage'. Nicolson wrote in March:

> Two months have not yet lapsed since Rebecca Loveridge destroyed hr child & attempted her own life by drowning, while in a state of insanity; no doubt largely due to the brutality of her husband. It would be inadvisable, not to say unkind, to speak of sending her back to him so soon.

Writing in June, Orange's view was that, 'Taking all the circumstances into consideration it would appear to be, on every ground, too soon to think of sending the poor woman back to her surroundings under which she broke down'. He also commented about Rebecca's state of mind: 'She is, at present, calm and rational, and orderly, and she appears to be deriving benefit from the rest and quietude that she is having.' Poor Rebecca: after years of abuse, overwork and repeated child-bearing, the relative peace of Broadmoor must have felt like a holiday. It is clear that the doctors running the asylum felt that she was better off there than with her husband.

In November, George wrote a letter to Orange asking for Rebecca to be discharged:

> I am pleased to send you these two notes of hand from the Revd Mr Jackson and John Whidborne, Esqre, as you

> requested me to get by the later end of this month. Sir I shall feel very thankful to you to name the day that I shall petition for my wife, I shall be home nearly all the winter as there are no horse fairs in this part until March, so I should be able to look after her all the winter myself and see how she gets on and every thing on Earth as I can do to make her comfortable, as long as I live, I will. I shall be thankful Sir to hear from you.

Given that George's ill-treatment was the cause of Rebecca ending up in Broadmoor, this took some chutzpah. One assumes that he was missing her contribution to looking after the horses as well as bringing up the children. John Whidborne, the local justice of the peace, wrote in support of George's request:

> I shall be glad to see Mrs Loveridge, who I understand from him is about to return to her home, monthly, and certify as to her state. But I am very confident that she will have every attention & kindness from her husband, and recommend her return to her home and family.

Whidborne's confidence seems misplaced.

Percival Jackson, the local vicar, also wrote in support, though it was voiced rather more cautiously: 'Should Mrs Loveridge return home I shall see her at her home constantly and shall be glad to give any report which may be desired of the impression which she gives as to her state of mind.'

In February 1885, Orange wrote to the Home Office:

> In compliance with your request to be furnished with a further report on the case of Rebecca Loveridge, I beg to say that the favourable condition of this patient existing

> in the [illegible] of your last when she was reported to be calm, rational and orderly, has been fully maintained without the occurrence of any relapse.
>
> She is, at present, in good bodily health, and is free from delusions, and does not suffer from either undue elevation or depression of spirits.
>
> He husband is very anxious to have her again at home; and she is very anxious to go; and, under all the circumstances, I think she might be allowed to do so, without incurring undue risk, her husband being quite willing to give the prescribed undertaking as set forth in the accompanying form.
>
> I enclose, also, for your consideration, three letters that I have received, one being from the husband, another from a Justice of the Peace, and two others from a clergyman.

By May, Orange was able to write in Rebecca's notes that she had 'gone on steadily & well since her reception, & has not shown any signs of active insanity since the date of last note'. In June, he wrote: 'Going on well in every respect.'

There were further exchanges of letters between Broadmoor and the Home Office. Everyone seemed to agree that it was a sad case, and that Rebecca was a good woman driven to insanity by her husband's cruel treatment. And yet Nicolson was able to write in September 1885 that Rebecca's condition was 'in every way satisfactory' and that 'I think that on the merits of the case itself she might be allowed to return to the care of her husband who has been most considerate & attentive to her during her confinement here'.

It seems unlikely that a man who had been so relentlessly abusive towards his wife could have overnight turned into someone who was genuinely considerate and attentive, and particularly surprising that a man like Nicolson, whose expertise was human psychology, could have believed it. Nonetheless, all seemed to agree that Rebecca could be released, and she was discharged in November 1885, less than two years after she'd been admitted. (A year later, a parcel arrived for Rebecca at Broadmoor, containing some apples and flowers, which were given to the asylum's infirmary. An accompanying note was forwarded to George. Frustratingly, we don't know who sent the parcel.)

After Rebecca returned to George, she lived a relatively long life, though it seems unlikely that it was a happy one. The couple continued to live at Oakford Farm, with George remaining in his job as a horse-dealer, and Rebecca taking responsibility for the dairy. In 1890, the eldest child, Rebecca, married a man named Charles Murrin, who worked as a labourer. Living at Oakford Cottage – probably a property connected to Oakford Farm – the couple had four sons and two daughters. Charles died in 1904 at the age of 36, but Rebecca lived to be 70.

At the time the 1891 census was taken, the other six children, ranging in age from 21 to 10, all still lived at the farm. In the next few years, three of the boys (George, John and Frederick) left home. George married a woman named Emily Maria and moved nearby to Brixham where he worked as a licensed victualler. They had one son. John too got married. He and his wife Sarah had two children and ran a smallholding together in Newton Abbott.

Henry, Rose and Florence remained at the farm, however. Henry helped out in his father's business, while Rose and Florence never married and worked alongside their mother in the dairy until well into their 30s. They eventually moved out and shared a house together in Powderham Road, Newton Abbot, where they remained until their deaths: Florence's in 1923, aged 42, and Rose's ten years later, aged 58.

While most of the siblings remained near home, Frederick struck out. In 1901 he enlisted as a private with the Imperial Yeomanry and was sent to South Africa to fight in the second Anglo-Boer War. He was discharged after three years.

George senior was to get in trouble with the law once more. In 1895, someone bought a horse from him for £20 – a mare that George had assured the buyer was sound and quiet both to ride and drive. The following day the new owner was driving the horse from Kingsteignton to Newton Abbot when the horse turned around twice without warning. It turned out that it was affected with a cataract of some months standing in the right eye – a condition that would eventually lead to blindness. George refused to have the horse back, and so the man sued him for £21. George claimed in court that he hadn't provided a warranty but the jury found for the plaintiff, awarding the full amount claimed as well as costs.[14]

Rebecca died in January 1922 at the age of 76. George outlived her by two years, dying in February 1924, aged 80. He left effects of more than £2,000 – a very substantial sum for someone who had spent much of his life as a peddler.

In Rebecca's story, we see something of the changing and sometimes contradictory attitudes of the late Victorian era: a woman who was trapped in an abusive marriage, which the state offered her no way of escaping, but who was also shown compassion when she committed the most horrific of crimes. We don't know what Rebecca's last years were like, but we can hope, unlikely though it seems, that after the publicity of the trial and the verdict, George behaved more gently towards his wife. Perhaps, too, she was able to find some pleasure in her old age in her children and grandchildren.

Chapter 7

Rebecca Turton

Rebecca Turton's story illustrates some of the difficulties facing historians researching the nineteenth century. Although she spent time in Broadmoor, she was born – and almost certainly died – in County Cork, Ireland. Birth, marriage and death records for that period are sparse, and complete census returns aren't available until 1901. That means that there are gaps in parts of Rebecca's story, and we might never find out exactly what brought her to London or how her life ended. She is also, it is fair to say, one of the less sympathetic characters in this book: as well as being a drunk, people generally found her difficult and unlikeable. Some inconsistencies in the record also suggest that on occasion she could be economical with the truth, making it even harder to piece her story together.

Rebecca Roberts was born in 1822 in Ireland, probably in Dunmanway, County Cork. Her father Christopher was a gunsmith – no doubt supplying the British army – and she also had a brother, Alexander, and a sister, but we don't know who her mother was. While it's been hard to trace anything of her early life, there is a tantalizing prison record showing that in September 1821, a Christopher Roberts, aged 28, had been arrested for 'firing shots with intent to murder at Dunmanway Fair'. The case was not prosecuted, but if, as seems likely, this was Rebecca's father, the criminal behaviour is of a piece with what we do know about her blood relatives.

There were no free schools in Ireland in the 1820s, but there were approximately 11,000 paying schools. It's possible that her family paid for her to attend one of these, at least briefly, because as an adult she was able to read and write, though imperfectly.

County Cork, like the rest of Ireland, was predominantly Catholic, but the Roberts family were Protestants. When the English conquered Ireland in the sixteenth century, thousands of English settlers flooded in, many of whom ended up in Cork. The religious divide was unbridgeable: inter-marriage, for example, was illegal, and the two communities didn't mix socially. By and large, Catholics lived in extreme poverty, with a meagre diet based on potatoes, while the small number of wealthy families and landowners was almost exclusively Protestant. This didn't mean that all Protestants were wealthy, however, and it is likely that Rebecca's family were of relatively modest means. A study of Protestants in County Waterford in the mid-nineteenth century has shown that by far the biggest number – a third of the total – were tradesmen, with jobs such as shoemaker and cabinet maker. There were also many, however, who lived in the kind of impoverished conditions endured by their Catholic neighbours.[1]

The 1820s and 1830s saw a combination of events that made life particularly difficult. Cork had been a major centre for supplying the British military effort in the Napoleonic wars, and had also provided men to join the army and navy. Once the wars were over, there was simultaneously both a collapse in the amount of work available and an influx of men who had fought for the British army. Small-scale industry (such as the weaving of coarse linens in West Cork) was in decline, which meant that thousands of former handloom workers now had to look for agricultural work. As a result of the deflation following the wartime boom, however, farmers had to cut their labour costs. In the 1830s, wheat growing began to decline while sheep farming (which required less labour) expanded. Wages for those who did manage to find work were pitifully low – a woman might be lucky to earn fourpence a day picking stones from pasture. There was a steep growth in unemployment and rural poverty.[2]

It's not surprising then that at some point Rebecca arrived in London, no doubt seeking work. The first potential sight we have of her is in the 1841 census, which shows a Rebecca Roberts living in 22 Rathbone Place, Marylebone and working as a servant: we can't be sure that this is the same Rebecca, but it seems likely, because it records that she was born in a different country. Seventeen months later, on 1 November 1842, she married Thomas Turton at the Church of St John the Evangelist, in Smith Square, two miles away. Her marriage certificate gives her trade as that of dressmaker. This isn't impossible – London had about 15,000 dressmakers in this period[3] – but it feels a little surprising. Dressmaking was a highly skilled job, though not a well-paid one, and it's not one that Rebecca could have done without training. On the same certificate, Thomas's job is given as engineer. More specifically, he was a boilermaker, whose job would have involved making boilers for steam engines, as well as other metal structures such as steam trains and steel ships. Thomas, who was eight years older, probably came from Yorkshire, and had arrived in London to look for work. His father John was a shoemaker.

In 1854, Rebecca and Thomas (known as 'Tom' to friends) were living at 1, Richard Street in Bromley in south-east London. At the time, particular trades were associated with different areas of London – Clerkenwell, for example, was home to the watchmaking and jewellery trades, while silk-weavers made their home in Spitalfields and Bethnal Green. The nearness to the dockyards meant that the easternmost part of London – places like Blackwall, Millwall, Poplar and Bromley – was populated by shipwrights, iron-founders and boilermakers.[4] At the time that Rebecca and Tom lived there, Bromley was a village, with only 4,000 inhabitants. (That changed with the coming of the railways just four years later.)[5] The house was tiny: only four rooms in total, as well as a kitchen. The Turtons occupied the two rooms on the first floor, using one as a sitting room and the other as a bedroom, with the landlord, William Owen Walker, and his wife living downstairs. None of them had lived there very long: at the time of the 1851 census, another family was living at the address.

The Walkers found Thomas to be a quiet neighbour, and they only heard the couple argue once. Rebecca, on the other hand, was 'very noisy', William Walker was later to testify, and 'disturbed everybody in the neighbourhood'. He described her as a 'perfect nuisance' who was 'almost continuously intoxicated' and 'was constantly abusing and jangling with her husband'. He once heard Rebecca tell her husband that he had been 'a whoring'. Rebecca was later to tell Broadmoor staff that she and Tom quarrelled frequently, because he was a drunk who taunted her for her Irishness and often threatened to have her committed to an asylum. She also claimed that Tom sometimes became so drunk that he fell over and injured himself. (It may be relevant that Tom also belonged to a friendly society, the Unity of Oddfellows, that met at the Volunteer pub. Members could pay in regular amounts that enabled a sum to be paid out on death: Rebecca would have been entitled to £10 when he died.) On Sunday, 16 April, Rebecca had been 'singing and dancing' so much that Walker's house had felt more like a public house than a private residential home.[6]

If Tom was a quiet drunk, and Rebecca was a noisy drunk, they were, nonetheless, both drunks. They also seem to have kept late hours. After midnight on the night of Thursday, 20 April, Rebecca came downstairs and told William that Thomas had taken arsenic. William called a policeman, George Pullen (spelt as Pulling in the Old Bailey transcript), to the house, who arrived at about 1.30 am. He was met by Rebecca, who repeated that Thomas had taken arsenic. Pullen accompanied Rebecca to the bedroom, and found Thomas lying asleep on the bed, fully clothed. He woke Thomas up and repeated what Rebecca had said, to which Thomas, who had been drinking, replied: 'I have not; I do not know what to do with my wife; she is going mad.' Pullen told Rebecca to go to bed and left the house. About twenty minutes later, he was passing the house again, and Rebecca opened the window and asked him, 'Are you the devil?' Pullen didn't reply, and Rebecca said (rather confusingly): 'The cats are scratching the graves open.' Pullen told her to shut the window and go to bed.

What happened next is pieced together from accounts given at the police court hearing, the inquest and the second Old Bailey trial. Some details of witnesses' stories changed between that first hearing and the second criminal trial more than a year later – but it's possible to create a timeline of events.

The following afternoon, at about 3 o'clock, both Rebecca and Tom visited Rebecca's friend Hannah Conner, a servant who lived with her parents in the upstairs rooms of 6, Batson Street. Hannah was to testify that there seemed to be a quarrel between them: Tom had been drinking and Rebecca was cross with him. She accused him of being with other women. While with Hannah, they drank half a pint of gin and some ale. They left together without making up their quarrel.

Rebecca and Tom seem to have parted ways after leaving Batson Street. She went to the house of her friend Rachel Green at 15, Alfred Street, who was married to James Green, a boilermaker who was probably a work colleague of Tom's. Rachel had known Tom seventeen years. When Rebecca arrived, she spoke to Rachel in a 'wild and incoherent manner', saying: 'Mrs Green, will you protect me, for there are four men on the bridge waiting to throw me over.' Rachel asked her to show her, and Rebecca took her outside and pointed to the bridge, but Rachel could see it was a delusion. Rebecca then added: 'Tom is going to kill me.' When Rachel remonstrated with her, Rebecca seemed jealous and told her that Tom was planning to marry another woman, adding: 'I am going to be murdered and cut up.'

James arrived home at about ten to six and found Rebecca there talking to his wife. He asked after Tom, and she told him that Tom had been 'ill using' her. She told James that the police and Tom had been hunting her with the intention of drowning her. 'Her talk was such that I considered she was either tipsy or mad,' he told the trial. He asked where Tom was, presumably with the intention of talking to him, but Rebecca took him back to Batson Street, arriving at about

8 o'clock. Rather than go up the stairs to Hannah's rooms, the pair went into the landlord's parlour downstairs. James left her at about 10 o'clock, and she went home.

Tom had arrived home earlier, and was let in by William. He had asked William the time, and William told him it was twenty past nine. He was a little the worse for wear – enough to affect his walking – but not excessively so. Having come home, he went out again, carrying a white jug to collect some beer. He arrived back a few minutes later, and let himself in with his own key.

About an hour after that, Rebecca arrived home – and at some point in the next two or three hours, she strangled her husband with one of his own trouser braces. She apparently did it so quietly that nobody heard her. At about 1 am, she came downstairs and asked William for the key to the front door. He told her where it was, and she went back to Batson Street to fetch Hannah who, not having gone to bed, was sitting up for her father (who was presumably ill). Rebecca knocked loudly twice on the door, and asked for Hannah's mother or father to accompany her home, because Tom was dead. Hannah's parents couldn't go, so Hannah accompanied her instead.

On the way, Rebecca told Hannah that she saw fairies and dead people at the side of the road and: 'Everything is double the size and all the people are going to the next world.' These comments made Hannah feel understandably frightened. When they arrived at the door, she told Hannah that 'poor Tom' was dead, and that she had killed him. William opened his own door and saw Hannah with Rebecca, who told him that Tom was dead. Ignoring this (perhaps assuming she was lying), William told Rebecca to go upstairs and not disturb him as she had done the night before. Once inside the Turtons' rooms, Hannah saw Tom lying dead and began to cry. She also noticed a broken pan on a chair in the bedroom, with a bloodstained brace in it, and a little water, 'as if something had been washed in it'. Rebecca took the pan off the chair, and emptied it into a pail on the landing. Hannah noticed a black handkerchief lying by Tom's side, 'twisted very much at the corner.' Rebecca picked it up and hung it on a nail behind the door, saying that it was the handkerchief that 'poor Tom' used to wear.

Meanwhile, William could hear Rebecca make a 'howling noise'. Then Hannah came downstairs and told him that Thomas was dead. Rebecca was still upstairs and William heard her cutting up wood to make a fire. He told Hannah to fetch a policeman or a doctor. It seems that Rebecca herself then went outside, where she was observed by George Pullen, who saw her standing at the corner of the street. Recognizing her, he asked her what the matter was. Initially she didn't answer, but on being asked again, she replied, 'My husband is dead.' The policeman accompanied her to the sitting room, at the front of the house, where he found Tom lying on the floor with a pillow under his head. The policeman noticed some marks on Tom's neck, and had a look around the room for more evidence, while Rebecca repeated, 'I did not do it, I did not do it!' Pullen noticed some tumblers and bottles, but Rebecca told him, 'It is no use your looking; I have not given him anything.'

Noticing that Tom wasn't wearing a neckcloth, Pullen asked Rebecca where it was. She claimed not to know, but Pullen found it hanging behind the sitting room door, with a shawl hung over it. Later Rebecca was to say that she had put it there and forgotten about it. Two doctors were called to the scene shortly afterwards: Ronald Robertson and a Mr Kennedy. It isn't clear whether they arrived together or separately.[7] Both gave similar evidence at trial. Robertson examined Thomas and found that his face was 'livid, and very much swollen, and the pupils of his eyes were distorted'. He also noted a 'broad livid mark round the neck, particularly under the left ear'. He added that 'the skin was abraded, as if a knot had been tied – all the external appearances were consistent with death by strangulation'. Later, he carried out a post mortem examination, which led him to the same conclusion. Kennedy concurred that Thomas had been strangled, either with the brace or with a handkerchief. He saw no signs of a struggle, and thought that Thomas had been drinking.

Pullen then took Rebecca to the police station. On the following Monday, he returned to the house and saw a bucket on the landing containing some wet clothes and a brace with a buckle on it. Pullen noticed that the buckle corresponded to the mark he had observed under Thomas's left ear. He then compared the buckle on the brace with the mark, and it was 'the same size, and fitted exactly'. (Presumably Thomas's body hadn't been moved.) He also found a corresponding buckle on Thomas's trousers. He was to show it to the surgeon carrying out the post mortem, who agreed that Thomas had been strangled by the brace.

The following morning, Rebecca was in her police cell when she was visited by a female searcher, Ann Randall. Rebecca asked if she could take the curling papers from her hair, and was told she could. She then asked for permission to pray, before kneeling and saying a prayer. When she got up, Randall asked her, 'Was your husband a good husband to you?' Rebecca replied, 'Very good when he was sober.' When Randall expressed the view that his death was a bad thing to have happened, Rebecca agreed: 'Certainly it was a bad thing, but what will not the devil tempt a person to do when they are in a passion?'

At the initial Thames police court (magistrates' court) hearing, Rebecca didn't give a favourable impression. A newspaper report described her as a 'stout, masculine-looking woman, by no means prepossessing in appearance'. Apparently, she remained calm and collected throughout the hearing, speaking in a low tone of voice that was at times almost inaudible. In a phrase that wouldn't be allowed under today's strict reporting conditions, the paper said that it was 'proved' that Rebecca 'had frequently abused her husband, and called him a beast and other vile names'. At the end of the hearing Rebecca was remanded on a charge of wilful murder and sent to Newgate gaol, a prison that had been in place since the twelfth century. (It was eventually closed in 1902.) It was a grim place: James Greenwood, a nineteenth-century writer who spent time there described his prison cell as 'the most wretched place that could be imagined', continuing:

> It was a very little place, with a window with an iron grate before it, and lime-washed walls, and a floor of asphalte. There were two shelves in the cell, one to stow the hammock away in the daytime, and the other to accommodate a tin pannikin, a copper bowl, a wooden spoon, and a wooden saltcellar, a piece of soap and a brush, the soap, though I don't know for what reason, being carried away at night and returned the next morning. Beside the furniture mentioned, there was a stool and a wooden flap hinged to the wall and propped with an iron crutch that served as a table. The hammock was a comfortable thing enough, and there were two sheets and two blankets. By-the-by, I mustn't forget the books – three in number – a Bible, a Prayer-book, and a Hymn-book, ranged in a row with the copper bowl and the other things.[8]

Food was sparse, consisting of meagre portions of bread and gruel for breakfast, and meat and potatoes, or meat soup and bread, for lunch. (In fairness, Greenwood describes the gruel and bread as 'very good'.) Prisoners had to clean their own cells using a dustpan and brush, and during the day they worked unpicking oakum (sorting out the fibres from old ropes, which could then be sold to ship-builders for mixing with tar to seal the lining of wooden craft), a job that was both manually difficult and immensely tedious. Prisoners also had to attend a chapel service daily.

The Newgate surgeon, Gilbert McMurdo, initially judged Rebecca insane. In May, she had a brief trial at the Old Bailey, where McMurdo gave evidence that he had seen Rebecca every day since she had been in prison and in his mind, she was 'undoubtedly insane'. He told the judge that he didn't think Rebecca was even aware that she had committed a murder, or been charged with the offence. Newgate's chaplain, the Reverend John Davis, said that he had repeatedly seen Rebecca labouring under delusions, telling him that her husband had rubbed her all over with white powder, and she also talked about having conversations with the devil. The jury returned a verdict that she was insane, and not in a condition to plead to the indictment, and she was detained at Her Majesty's Pleasure.

In June, she was moved to Bethlem Hospital, the insane asylum, and then returned to Newgate. (Rebecca was later to tell Broadmoor staff that she was sent to Fisherton House, not Bethlem, but contemporary records show differently.)

In her second stay at Newgate, McMurdo decided that Rebecca no longer showed signs of insanity: he conversed with her on a number of subjects, and although she claimed not to remember killing Tom, she 'conversed very well' on other topics and McMurdo thought her fit to plead. Her second trial at the Old Bailey took place in August 1855, sixteen months after Thomas was strangled. McMurdo gave evidence that, while he considered Rebecca sane enough to plead, he also believed her to have been insane when he first saw her. On this basis, no doubt, the jury found Rebecca not guilty, on the grounds of insanity, and she was detained at Her Majesty's Pleasure.

Broadmoor hadn't opened at this stage, so Rebecca was taken back to Bethlem, before being transferred in February 1856 to the criminal wing of Fisherton House in Salisbury, where she was to spend the next seven years.

Fisherton, founded in 1813, was the largest private mental hospital in England. At any one time, it housed about 300 or 400 patients, and was one of the principal asylums taking criminal lunatics. We know a little of what Fisherton was like from William Gilbert, an assistant poor law commissioner, who published an account of his visit to it in 1864. Gilbert wrote that the asylum was 'like a village. It comprises many houses, some very large … They are separated by high walls, so that the patients may be divided according to their cases and the accommodation they require'.[9]

Of the main hospital building, he wrote that it 'resembled a remarkably handsome villa … and the beautifully arranged grounds favoured the illusion'. On the occasion he visited, the asylum was holding a ball for patients, which took place in a grand ballroom, with a twelve-strong band of musicians playing. The patients were all dressed up for the occasion, though the richer patients were better-turned out than the poorer ones. Many of the women wore paper flowers, which they had made themselves. Gilbert was shocked to discover that many of the patients, who all behaved impeccably, were convicted criminals, some of them murderers. On being given a guided tour of the asylum, he was surprised to be told by the principal, Dr Lush, that he did not need harsh measures to keep order: 'I have not a pair of handcuffs, or a lock-up cell, or any instrument of punishment whatever, in the whole establishment.' Instead, he said, he maintained order 'principally by kindness, and a very powerful staff of warders'. He added, 'As lunatics, they have not the intelligence for combination in a plot,' which must have been reassuring.

The patients themselves were housed in dormitories. Gilbert was impressed by what he saw: the dormitory he visited was 'well ventilated and light' and the room was 'scrupulously clean, the walls were whitewashed and hung with coloured prints illustrative of various events in Holy Writ and in history, ancient and modern.' All in all, Fisherton 'had more the appearance of a well-regulated hospital than that of either prison or lunatic asylum'.[10]

Dr Lush also gave Gilbert some insight into the psychology of the criminal lunatics, telling him: 'I never met with a case in which a genuine repentance was visible in a person who had in a fit of insanity killed another.'[11]

Fisherton may have been a model of patient care, but it seems its security left something to be desired. When Rebecca had been there two years, she witnessed a murder. One Saturday morning, at about breakfast time, she looked out into the airing ground and saw one of her fellow patients, Catherine Clarke, attack another patient, Mary Kenney, striking her hard with a flat iron. At the inquest, she described seeing Clarke, who was only 17, hit Kenney as though using a dagger, and once she fell forward, kick her in the head and strike her again with the iron. Rebecca then called out to a staff member, Mrs Day, and the two women ran out, Rebecca prising the iron out of Clarke's hands. She then asked Clarke – who had apparently been threatening to kill Mary Kenney for some time – why she had done it, and Clarke replied that people talked to her from the clouds, and that Kenney was the reason she was being kept confined. The inquest jury decided that Clarke was insane at the time of the murder.[12]

In 1863, however, Rebecca transferred to the newly opened Broadmoor. Her bodily health on arrival was 'good', and by this point she had no delusions or obvious evidence of insanity. Fisherton staff told Broadmoor that she had been at times 'restless, grumbling and quarrelsome'.

When she arrived at Broadmoor, the only other patients were female: the men didn't arrive until February 1864. Numbers initially were small, and by the end of 1864, the asylum still only housed ninety-five women and 214 men.

At Broadmoor, the impression of her was that she was a 'tall stout woman, sallow complexion, dark hair inclining to grey, hazel eyes, a somewhat odd manner though shewing no signs of positive delusion'. She also had an 'intermittent pulse' and suffered from 'dyspepsia and heartburn'.

It was impossible to know how much Rebecca remembered of her crime. She knew that she had been accused of strangling her husband with a brace but said that she didn't think she had done so. She was clearly not well liked at the asylum. In December of the year she was admitted she was described as being able to 'talk rationally enough' but 'inclined to be discontented and fault finding'. Moreover: 'Her manner is often very irritating to her companions and although she can control herself when she chooses, she often makes a great deal of mischief with her tongue.' Later she is described as having an 'irritating perverse manner but is free from delusions'. Sometimes she would pretend to have forgotten the details of her crime, but the superintendent, John Meyer, was unconvinced: 'From her manner it is probable that she remembers the circumstances quite well.'

As time passes, the notes carry on in the same vein. She shows 'no indication of insanity' but 'is of rather a quarrelsome disposition'. Asked in July 1864 whether she remembers her husband's death, she replies 'Certainly not'. Apparently, she 'seems to think that the worst feature in her case is her own position, the predicament in which she found herself'. She 'has no adequate appreciation of the crime committed – blames her husband – says he was so addicted to drink that he did not take care of her'. Later, she 'generally wears the air of a much injured person', though, on the plus side she 'works well at her needle'. (If Rebecca really had been a dressmaker, as claimed on her marriage certificate, this would explain her proficiency at needlework.)

Over the next few years, Rebecca was described variously as 'behaving very well lately', of appearing 'sullen and dissatisfied without any apparent cause', of 'occasional moodiness' and of being 'particularly well behaved and orderly for the last few months'. After three or four years in Broadmoor, she was showing no signs of insanity and was working in the laundry. However, she still wasn't very well liked: by 1869, although she was described as being generally 'quiet and well behaved', she also 'makes mischief with other patients', is 'very heartless' and has 'no appreciation of her crime'.

Despite all this, it was obvious that Rebecca by now was perfectly sane, and so arrangements were made to discharge her. Broadmoor authorities were always reluctant to discharge someone without a family member to look after them, which meant that Rebecca would have to go back to Ireland. The obvious candidate to take care of her was her brother, Alexander Robertson, who lived in

Clonakilty, a market town in County Cork. Contemporary trade directories suggest a flourishing town filled with haberdashers, milliners, saddlers and stationers, as well as more than forty public houses. Alexander wrote to Meyer in July saying: 'I am most happy to receive her, and will do all in my power to support her.' Perhaps, as her brother, he was a little more tolerant of her foibles than the Broadmoor staff and patients.

The absence of birth and census records means that we know very little about Alexander. A commercial directory shows an Alexander Robertson working as a nailmaker in Clonakilty in 1871, which sounds promising – but he is still listed in 1881, by which time, according to Rebecca's account, he had been dead for nine years. Someone by the same name, who had been born in Dunmanway (about fifteen miles from Clonakilty) was found not guilty of stealing nine shillings and sixpence in 1861, aged 35. This Alexander, who had been held in Cork Prison, was 5 feet 10½ inches tall, with a sallow complexion, hazel eyes and black hair. He was also a nailmaker, so there's a good chance that this is the same person who had the business in Clonakilty. But we can't be sure it was Rebecca's brother.

At any rate, in August 1869, a member of staff accompanied Rebecca to Cork. She was to be directed into the care, not of Alexander, but of her nephew, David Burleigh, in Dunmanway. Burleigh was almost certainly the son of Rebecca's sister (whose name we don't know) and her husband, Robert Burleigh. Dunmanway itself was a small town with a population of 2,738 in 1841, which probably shrank after the emigrations caused by the Great Famine.

We know more about David Burleigh than any other member of Rebecca's family. This is down to the remarkably detailed records kept by Cork Prison, which show that a David Burleigh, born in 1849 in Innishannon and living in Dunmanway – almost certainly Rebecca's nephew, in other words – had numerous spells in prison (in 1874, 1875, 1876, 1879, 1880, 1882, 1888, 1896, 1899, 1901, 1902), usually for being drunk and disorderly, but on one occasion for 'trespass in pursuit of game', on another for 'stealing clothing' and another for committing assault.

As with Alexander Robertson, Burleigh's prison record gives a detailed description of his appearance: 5 feet 8½ inches tall, stout, brown hair, blue eyes, arched eyebrows, a long nose, a fresh complexion (surprising, given the drink), an oval face and scars on each shin from being kicked. It also provides details of his job: he was a whitesmith (a term for a metalworker) and, like Alexander, a nailer. In 1876, Burleigh married Mary Good, but by 1901, now aged 61, he was widowed, living in Innishannon and still working as a whitesmith.

All in all, Burleigh might not have been the best person to take care of Rebecca, and indeed her life went downhill rapidly after she arrived home in County Cork. It had changed in important respects since she left as a young woman. The Great Famine of 1845–51 had hit hard, and thousands of people had emigrated. Later, various agricultural crises led to yet more people emigrating, mostly to the US. Some of those who were left were sustained by funds sent by relatives abroad – though on the plus side a lack of agricultural labour also meant that those who remained were able to command higher wages. This is relative, of course: the majority of people were still very poor, and most agricultural work was on a casual basis. A badly thought-out change to poor-law regulations, which proved costly for rural landlords, meant that most labourers now had to live in the towns, often in insanitary conditions, and travel long distances to work.[13]

We can piece together some of what happened to Rebecca from a series of letters she wrote to Orange. Now going by the name Rebecca Roberts or sometimes Robertson, she frequently found herself short of funds and was forced to write in desperation to the one person who might be in a position to help. Fortunately, Broadmoor had a fund to help former patients.

The first letter in her file is dated November 1870, but as it thanks Orange for a gift of stamps (in lieu of money), it suggests she has previously written to him asking for financial help. (One oddity, given Rebecca's Protestantism, is that the letter is written on notepaper headed with a poem on an Irish nationalist theme. It may have been all she could get hold of.) This is the letter, complete with Rebecca's distinctive spelling:

> Hoping that you will parding my neglect in not Leting you know earlier that receaved your kind letter and the stamps and am truly thankful to your Honner for your kindness in time of need. Sir my nephew had to go home for change of air it was a very Bad pluracy that he had And you may think how bad off it was all the tim that he was away he is come back. Last week he is doing as well as he can at present for he is not very strong et for you know there is not much nourichment for poor pepol in this Contry. I wish that I never came to thos place but must try and mak the best of it now hoping at the turn of Chrismas to have thing better with God's help then it will return your great kindness.

She concludes by asking Orange to give her good wishes to Mrs Orange and the children, and in a sad postscript writes: 'I am allmost bare foot.'

In August 1871, Rebecca wrote again to Orange in clear distress. She wrote that one nephew had enlisted, while the other had got married. He and his wife had gone away and left Rebecca 'quite destituted'. With nowhere to live, she was relying on the kindness of a neighbour, a boot- and shoemaker named Mr O'Sullivan, to give her a place to sleep until she could find some work. (This would have been Jeremiah Sullivan, who, records show, ran a boot- and shoemaking business on Dunmanway's Main Street.) She once again asks for money in order to be able to find some work:

> If I had the prise of some Appels and biscuts I would attend the market and fairs to try and get my living for I am in want of cloths and vetils [clothes and vittles, or food]. When I get up in the morning I do not know where to get my breakfast, only a litel from one and another.

A note underneath records that the asylum sent her five stamps.

In September, she wrote a thank you letter to Orange, informing him that his gift had enabled her to go to the fair and make eight shillings (it's not clear how, but perhaps she was able to sell some goods), with which she had bought some clothes. She had found a job nursing an old lady called Mrs Sanders, who lived at Underhill Cottage, for £6 a year plus board. It was, however, a demanding job that involved working all day and staying up much of the night.

Three years later, in September 1874, Rebecca wrote again to Broadmoor. She was now living in Innishannon, a village some twenty miles from Dunmanway. After inquiring about the health of her fellow patients and Mrs Jackson (the same staff member to whom Mary Ann Meller's husband sent a letter), she says that one of her sister's sons who had been kind to her (this may have been the one who enlisted) had died two years earlier, while the other had married and gone to Wales. She had been working somewhere for £4 a year (this may have been the job nursing Mrs Sanders), but the work was so hard she had developed rheumatics, which had caused her to leave her position. She was now lodging with her sister for free, but her sister had 'so many littel children and not much to give them' that she had very little to spare for Rebecca. She concludes by saying that she is about to start a new position, but is short of clothes and boots, and asks Orange for 'a few shillings'. She says that if he is willing to help,

'I would never troubel you agane with God's help, hoping that God will pay you doubley'.

In response, Orange sent her five stamps.

Rebecca was to write two more letters to Orange. In June 1878, she wrote from her sister's house in Innishannon explaining that she had been working in a gentleman's house 'a long way below Cork' and that there was so much hard work that she was obliged to leave in bad health. Her brother had been dead six years, and her only friend was her 'poor sister' who was 'very bad off' because she had such a large family. Once more she asks for two or three shillings so that she could go to Cork to look for a position. Underneath the letter is a handwritten note from Orange stating that he has 'no fund' to send her any relief.

The last letter is dated December 1879. Rebecca writes from Main Street, Dunnanway, though it's not clear whether she is once more staying with the O'Sullivans or somewhere else. It is a heart-rending letter, which recounts that she is almost barefoot and has had to pawn her shawl in order to be able to afford two meals a day. Without the kindness of people who have given her free lodgings, she doesn't know how she could live. There is no work, and people in Ireland are 'so bad off' that they are 'half-starve'. Once more she asks for some money and promises not to ask again. She concludes by wishing God's blessing on him and his family. After that, there is no more: we can't be sure that Rebecca didn't end her days in Dunmanway's workhouse, a grim place to be avoided at all costs.

What we don't know, of course, is how reliable a narrator Rebecca is. Was she poor because she had no work, or because she drank her earnings? Did she leave her jobs because the heavy work was making her ill, or because her employers had had enough of her? Did the brother tasked with taking care of her really die three years after she arrived home? There are so many unanswered questions, but whatever the truth of the matter, it seems that Rebecca ended her life destitute.

Chapter 8

Julia Spickernell

Julia Spickernell's life was very different from many of the other women in this book. She was born into, and, for the most part, remained a member of, the lower-middle class: although never affluent, she did not experience the same kinds of financial struggles as those experienced by working-class women. Yet even well-off women were susceptible to the burdens of repeated childbearing and infant mortality, and the circumstances that led to Julia's spell in Broadmoor were similar to those experienced by women such as Mary France and Elizabeth White.

Georgiana Julia Edwards was born in Aston, Hertfordshire, a small rural village (with a population of 639 in 1872)[1] on 2 August 1852, and baptized on 2 January 1853. In later records, her first names are usually given as Julia Georgiana or Julia Georgianna. Her father, William Henry, had been born in Barton, Bedfordshire, while her mother, Elizabeth, was from Aston.

By the time of her birth, her parents already had three older children, shown in the 1851 census as Ann, aged 6; Thomas, 4; and William, 1. At the time, east Hertfordshire was dominated by arable farming, with more men employed in farm work than in any other sector.[2] William senior, however, ran a sweetshop, and the family was well off enough to employ a single domestic servant, Mary Smith, then aged 12.

Ten years later, circumstances had changed. The family was now living fifteen miles away in the parish of Wormley, another tiny Hertfordshire village, close to Broxbourne, with a population of only 579 in 1872. Julia's older brothers were working as farm labourers, while her father, now aged 41, was a police officer, and Julia and her younger brother, George, aged 7, were still in school. The region's agrarian economy offered limited opportunities for female employment,[3] and Ann had left the family home to work as a domestic servant for Elizabeth's brother, William Chalkley, a corn merchant in Stevenage.

We don't know what brought about the family's change of circumstances, but perhaps William's business failed and he had to take a waged position. By middle-class standards, wages were on the low side – William probably earned about twenty shillings a week. Nonetheless, a police constable at the time was a respectable working-class job, with, according to the historian David Taylor, 'security of employment, regularity of pay and variety of fringe benefits'.[4]

By 1871, Julia had a new sibling, 9-year-old Harriet, who had been born in Wormley. The family was living at the Knight Street Police Station in Sawbridgeworth, Hertfordshire, the accommodation being a perk of William's job. Thomas, now 23, was a labourer engaged in the malting process. The family also had two lodgers: 70-year-old Jane Carter, a widow, and Esther Roberts, 54, a dressmaker. The 18-year-old Julia Edwards, as she was now known, was working as a domestic servant with the family of William Manley, a merchant, in Broxbourne.

In September that same year, Julia's father, William, died, at the age of 52, of confluent smallpox – a victim of the last great smallpox pandemic to affect the UK, in which about 42,000 people died over two years.[5] The introduction of vaccination earlier in the century meant that fewer people died in the UK than elsewhere, though that would have been small consolation to William's family. Confluent smallpox was a particularly nasty variant of the disease in which the smallpox blisters merged into a single sheet, detaching the outer layers of skin from the flesh underneath.

Between her father's death, and her wedding seven years later, Julia moved to London. She was living in Holborn, at 6, Gray's

Inn Passage – a road that no longer exists, but at the time was a passageway between what is now Sandland Street and Red Lion Square. Census records show that the house was typically occupied by two or more families at any one time, usually of tradesmen. Julia's presence there is a puzzling, unless she was working as a servant to one of the families.

Her new spouse, Frederick Henry Spickernell, was a clerk, also living in Holborn, at 21, Great James Street. They were married at their local church, St Andrew's. It was a church with historical associations: rebuilt by Christopher Wren after the Great Fire of London, it was where Benjamin Disraeli was received into the Christian Church.[6] On the certificate, Julia's father's job is recorded as confectioner, rather than police officer – maybe she felt her father's earlier position to be a more accurate reflection of her social status. The witnesses to the marriage were Julia's sister Harriet, and David Childs, probably another relative.

We can't be quite sure what brought Julia to London, but it was likely to have been work. (Harriet too, by the early 1880s, was working as a servant in Marylebone, probably in a similar role.) According to her Broadmoor case notes, Julia had been working as a lady's maid before marriage – this was a live-in role and doesn't quite tally with the Gray's Inn Passage address. A cut above other domestic servant roles, a lady's maid would attend to her mistress's personal needs, such as mending her clothes or arranging her hair (something Mrs Beeton described as 'the most important part of a lady's-maid office')[7], while the more menial tasks of cleaning and dusting were left to housemaids. Usually, a young woman employed as a lady's maid would come from a slightly better-off background than other domestic servants: she would be expected to be able to read and write as well as sew and dress hair.

Frederick had been born in Oxfordshire in 1852 to James, 36 and Martha, 27. The couple had married in 1848, and before Frederick's birth they were living with their 2-year-old daughter Jane in the household of Conrad Owen, an army major, where James was a domestic servant. Within ten years, however, the family had moved to Berriew, Montgomeryshire, and James was working as a land agent. By now, they had three more children: James, born in 1854, Alfred, born in 1847 and Emily, born in 1861. James (the child) died not long after Emily was born.

By 1871, the family had moved again, and James and Martha were now employed as officers in the Henley Union Workhouse. Frederick, however, is untraceable in the 1871 census, so we don't know how he came to be in London or start work as a clerk.

In October 1880, when Julia gave birth to the couple's first child, Emily Violet, the couple were living at 19, Devonshire Street, Islington. They exemplified a new breed of middle-class couple, who migrated from their home towns and villages to London, where the population quadrupled from under one million in 1801 to almost four million in 1881.[8]

Islington was an area where the population was growing particularly fast, increasing from 10,212 residents in 1801 to 319,143 in 1891.[9] It was also socially mixed, drawing in the wealthier middle classes, the new white-collar workers and poorer families who had been displaced by the railway building programme in inner London.

Frederick's job made him part of that band of white-collar workers. Although many of us think of the Victorian period as a time when everyone rigidly kept to their place in the class system, the wealth of new job opportunities made it much more socially mobile than earlier eras. By 1881, there were 58,278 male commercial clerks in London,[10] many of whom were upwardly mobile: marriage records from the late nineteenth century show that about 40 per cent of clerks had working-class fathers.[11] In fact, the historian Jason Long has compared census data relating to fathers and sons that suggests the rate of upward mobility may have been even higher.[12] Socially, clerks were in a difficult position: they were keen to differentiate themselves from manual workers, but their aspirations and snobbery made them a target of parody, most notably in the character of the Grossmiths' Charles Pooter, whose social faux pas were documented in a column in *Punch*.[13]

Telegraph clerk was a job skilled enough to have required some training and, while not as well paid as professional middle-class jobs, was more secure than traditional working-class occupations – and, of course, considerably less physically arduous. In one sense, clerks were hard to place socially. As Gregory Anderson points out, there were 'innumerable gradations of clerks covering a very wide spectrum of ability, career prospects, job type, status and remuneration'.[14] Their wages varied enormously, though most junior clerks seem to have earned less than £100 a year. Despite the wide difference between the lowest and highest earners, they could nonetheless be seen as a homogenous group. In his book *The Blackcoated Worker*, David Lockwood describes them in economic terms as 'sometimes on the margin' but socially 'definitely part of the middle class. They were so regarded by the outside world, and they regarded themselves as such'.[15]

Frederick wasn't just a clerk: he was working in a cutting-edge technology that was expanding rapidly. Telegraphy was one of the great inventions of the Victorian age, transforming business by allowing rapid communication over great distances. Its use was limited until the development of a technology in the late 1850s called the Universal Private Telegraph that made it possible for private individuals and organizations (banks, police stations, government offices, domestic residences and so on) to connect with each other. A person in one place could type out a message that then travelled down the wire to someone else, say, twenty miles away. According to Andrew Wynter, writing in 1865, Londoners had begun using them to book theatre tickets; husbands were telegraphing wives to let them know they were bringing a friend home for dinner. When different telegraph cables were connected to each other, even greater things were possible, Wynter wrote:

> By combining beforehand different lines in this manner, two different persons may converse together across the island, sitting in their own drawing-rooms; nay, by only extending the connection of these lines with the submarine cables across the sea, a person may converse with his friend travelling day by day at the other end of the globe, provided only that he keeps on some telegraphic line that is continuous with the main electric trunk-lines of the world. This may appear to be an idle dream, but that it will certainly come to pass we have no manner of doubt whatever.[16]

One of the features of the new middle class was a different approach to family life. Both Julia and Frederick were now living some distance from their parents. Julia's mother, Elizabeth, remained in Hertfordshire: in 1881, she was living with her nephew Edward Lewin and his wife Julia. Julia Lewin's brother Henry Rose, a pork butcher, and his wife Mary, were also living with them, as was Edward's 5-year-old cousin Walter Childs. Edward's income, according to the census record, 'derived from houses', suggesting a family who were comfortably off. Frederick's parents remained in Henley, where his father was now superintendent of labour at the workhouse.

Compared to their working-class contemporaries, the Spickernells lived in relatively spacious accommodation, particularly later in their marriage. The new middle class, argues Geoffrey Crossick, had different boundaries between family and social life from the working class:

> The availability of space in the lower middle class home allowed a family centredness, a degree of privacy and isolation that was impossible for most working class families who consequently spilled into the street, the public house, the external entertainment. It was also the

> individualistic ideology of the lower middle class that drove them inwards into the security of a family life that was often incapable of bearing the strains imposed upon it.[17]

Yet although removed from her mother, Julia remained close to her sister, so she was not without family support. But one experience that united middle-class and working-class women was the strain of repeated child-bearing, combined, very often, with the death of children in infancy.

Like Mary Ann Meller, Julia adopted the new trend, particularly popular amongst middle-class women, of having a doctor attend her birth. Doctors were keen to attend births because it enabled them to forge a continuing bond with families that would last for the long term. From women's point of view, the medical profession's eventual adoption of chloroform to reduce childbirth pain would have been a good reason to hire a doctor.[18] This was particularly true for Julia, who was to have six babies in eight years. Emily Violet was followed by Frederick James (1882), Alfred George (1883), Maude Mary (1884), Edith Florence (1886) and Mabel Constance (1888). Neither Alfred nor Maude lived for very long, Alfred dying of diarrhoea at only ten weeks, and Maude of acute bronchitis at three months. In 1885, the family was in lodgings at 128, Shakespeare Road, Stoke Newington, paying a rent of 7s 6d a week for the first floor and breakfast parlour, unfurnished. They were still there when Edith was baptized in May 1886. The burden of bearing, and then caring for, so many children, and then losing them to illness, must have taken a heavy toll on Julia.

Socially, however, the Spickernells were on the up. By 1888, the family had moved to 93, Milton Street – a three-storey house in Stoke Newington with a basement room that was rented out to another clerk and his wife. Fred was by now employed as a telegraphist by the Submarine Telegraph Company,[19] a prosperous business and the first in the world to lay an undersea telegraph cable, which ran all the way from Cornwall to America.[20] Although the inland telegraph companies had been nationalized in 1870, becoming part of the General Post Office (GPO), those operating internationally were exempted – though Frederick did later join the GPO. The growing importance of the telegraph for doing business made it a particularly secure job.

It was Milton Road where, in December 1888, Julia committed the crime that was to send her to Broadmoor. Julia had been experiencing pains in her head and back and complained of feeling 'very peculiar'. Although she was looking forward to a visit from her mother, she was also worried about 9-month-old Mabel's bronchitis. On Christmas Eve, she went into the kitchen to wash a nightdress belonging to one of the children. Frederick told her not to, because she might catch a chill. She then 'flew at his throat' and said, 'Oh Fred, I will murder you; I will murder you and then I shall be a murderess.'[21]

A few days later, on 29 December, Julia told Mary Ann Goldring, the neighbour in the basement, that she had to scrub down the stairs because a portion of the ceiling had fallen on it. Mrs Goldring told her not to worry herself with it because her servant would help her later on. She took Julia's three older children into her own flat to look after them. Left alone, Julia filled a bucket of warm water to clean the stairs. She then picked up Mabel, placed her in the bucket, and drowned her.

Having killed her baby, Julia knocked on Mary Ann's door and told her she had something to show her and that she must come immediately, and bring her servant Ada. When Mary Ann and Ada arrived at the kitchen door, Julia said, 'I have done it!' Mary Ann, who said that Julia 'appeared excited and had her dress unfastened at the neck', replied, 'You are excited; done what?' Julia answered: 'Give me Mr Goldring's razors' and then screamed.[22]

Mary Ann, understandably alarmed, ran out of the house to call the next-door neighbour, Lucy Cavalier, and to send for the local doctor,

Edward Spencer. Lucy knocked at Julia's bedroom door, and Julia invited her in. Lucy gave an account of what happened next at Julia's trial:

> I sat her on a box by the side of the drawers, and she said, 'I have done it; the devil made me do it; he has been following me about up and down stairs the last five weeks' – I asked her what was troubling her – she said the work had been troubling her a great deal; she tried to do the work and could not – she seemed very excited – after a few minutes she got quieter, and I then went into her room; I there found the child in a pail of water placed head downwards, and covered by the water; I took it out and laid it on the bed – it was fully dressed.

When Dr Spencer arrived at 11 am, Mary Ann returned to her own flat. Going upstairs to the top rooms, Spencer found Julia in a very agitated state. She ran forward with outstretched hands, 'as if', the newspaper report said, 'with the intention of clutching at witness's throat'. She apparently 'spoke snatches of sentences in a wild and incoherent manner at the top of her voice, and was evidently in a condition of great mental motion'.

Spencer said that he understood her to say she wanted a rope to hang herself with. Then she flew at him, 'holding out both her hands, as if in the act of clutching me by the face or throat'. He took her by both hands and she partly fell and he partly threw her to the ground, where he held her until she became quieter. He took her to the front bedroom, where he placed her on a chair and Julia asked for a rope to hang herself. Leaving her in the charge of the two women, Spencer went to the back backroom where he saw Mabel lying on the bed, her clothes 'warm from the warm water in the bucket'. He believed the 'whole body had been put in the water' and observed 'no marks of violence on the body'.

The newspaper report of Julia's initial hearing at Dalston Police Court, on the same day, expanded further on Spencer's testimony:

> Death was, in witness's opinion, due to drowning. There was an ordinary household pail three-parts filled with water in the same room, and he thought that the child had been placed bodily in this. The doctor added that he had known the family for some years. Mrs Speckernell [*sic*] had always been a good, kind mother. She had been nursing this child, and it was just possible that it might have upset the poor woman's mind. She was certainly insane when witness first saw her.[23]

Spencer told the court that he had always found her to be 'very fond of the children'.

Shortly afterwards, a policeman arrived at the scene. According to Mary Ann Goldring's servant, Ada Baldwin, Julia asked the police constable 'for a rope with which to hang herself, or a razor to cut her head open'.

Julia was not called to enter a plea at this initial hearing, because Dr Spencer said she was not in a fit state to make a statement. At the end of her initial hearing, Julia was then remanded to prison for a week. The newspaper report poignantly concludes:

> She was taken away a few minutes later in a cab. The husband, who seemed deeply moved at what had occurred, wished to bid her an affectionate farewell. She declined at first, saying that she was a murderess, and then she assented.

At the inquest into Mabel's death, Dr Spencer testified that he had 'always found Mrs Spickernell a careful and fond mother. He had never attended her except for her confinements'. The jury found that Mabel had been drowned by Julia, who at the time 'was not responsible for her actions'. The coroner made out a commitment for 'wilful murder' against Julia.[24]

Under cross-examination at the Old Bailey trial in February, Spencer acted both as character witness and medical expert. He had attended her during some of her confinements and described her as a 'kind and affectionate mother'. As Julia was 'still suckling her child', he thought her 'mania' arose from 'over-lactation', explaining further:

> There are three kinds of puerperal mania: one which comes on in the puerperal state before the child is born, another which comes on during the state of labour or soon after, and another kind which is recognized as the insanity of lactation; she was still suckling her child at this time – it is common to get this condition in women of delicate constitution, who have borne children rapidly, and have a profuse supply of milk, especially after loss of rest or anything likely to exhaust the nervous system – pain in the head is one of the symptoms that would occur.

The detail that Julia was normally a 'kind and affectionate mother' is a significant one in helping determine that she was acting out of insanity rather than cruelty. Like Spencer, the police surgeon, Thomas Jackman, expressed the view that, having examined and questioned Julia, he had 'found her state of mind to be undoubtedly insane'. He added that 'homicidal mania occasionally arises from over-secretion of milk; no doubt in this case it was so – I formed the opinion that she was incapable of appreciating the nature and quality of the act she did'.

Philip Francis Gilbert, medical officer of Holloway Prison, who saw Julia on 30 December, also 'formed the opinion that she was insane'. Describing her as 'intensely dejected' he went on:

> She took no notice of her surroundings; she was moaning and rocking herself to and fro; it was with difficulty I could make her speak; when she did, she sobbed and said she had been an extremely wicked woman, that she had gone through hell, that she had been a wicked wretch all her life, and was unfit to live – besides this, she was under the delusion that she heard a voice that came from the devil, continually accusing her of doing nothing but taking care of herself.

She also complained of 'intense headache' and a voice keeping her awake at night accusing her of self-indulgence. What he saw, Gilbert added, 'was consistent with a form of insanity arising from excessive lactation'. He also mentioned that her husband and sister 'state that they have noticed her very low & depressed since about the end of November 88 & she has spoken to sister about her unworthiness. Was a devoted & affectionate Mother'. He concluded by saying that the bout of mania had passed, and that Julia was 'mentally recovered' and 'shows no indication whatever of insanity now'.

Discussing Julia's case in the context of Victorian ideas about criminal responsibility, an academic lawyer called Nicola Lacey has argued that the three doctors 'tailored their evidence carefully to the doctrinal requirements of the McNaghten Rules'. The head pains reported by Julia 'reflected the prevailing idea of insanity as physically located in the brain'. But this view that Julia was temporarily deranged was at odds, Lacey suggests, with the witness testimony that shows that Julia was aware of what she had done, and with Julia's own claim that she was 'extremely wicked'.[25]

The case gives rise to difficult questions about personal responsibility, Lacey argues: 'The gap between someone who "just couldn't help themselves" and someone who "failed to understand what they were doing" is perilously fine – as Julia Spickernell's case illustrates.'

The real problem, surely, is with the law's narrow definition of insanity that says a person can only be found insane if they had no idea what they were doing. Julia seems to have known what she was doing, and to have known it was wrong, but also, in common with some of the other women in this book, to have been unable to stop herself.

As David Nicolson pointed out, however, juries tended not to get bogged down in fine distinctions of responsibility,[26] and Julia was found 'guilty, but insane', which had replaced the earlier 'not guilty by reason of insanity' verdict – though the effect was the same. She was admitted to Broadmoor shortly after her trial, one of twelve women admitted in 1889. During her time there, she would probably have met two of the other women in this book: Mary France and Elizabeth White.

It seems to have been a less happy year than usual for the asylum. Of the fifty-four patients admitted, twenty-two were convicts. This increased the proportion of 'restless, turbulent and viciously disposed inmates' and they showed 'a greater readiness to proceed to acts of insubordination and violence'.[27] Nicolson's solution was to house the convicts away from other patients, but he himself once more had the misfortune to be concussed when one threw a heavy stone at his head. The inspectors, however, were largely satisfied, finding the patients to be in good health, the food satisfactory and plenty to occupy patients: 'No lack of papers, books, and means of amusement was apparent in the wards, and the associated amusements are varied and sufficiently frequent.'[28]

Julia's admission record from Holloway Prison describes her bodily health as 'indifferent' and mentions that the attack of insanity had lasted two months. The cause of the insanity was 'lactation' and 'ill health'. Although her education is 'imperfect', she could read and write 'fairly well' and was of temperate habits. Repeating the description of Julia's delusion as hearing a 'voice from the devil, continuously accusing her of self indulgence', the record says that Julia 'began to improve mentally about Jan 7th and now is recovered.'

The record also says that Julia had spoken to Harriet 'about her unworthiness'. It notes, however, that she 'was a devoted and affectionate mother'.

Julia's file contains a handwritten note with additional information provided by Frederick, stating that Julia had recovered from her confinement, but that she was weakened from suckling the baby – an indication that Frederick had grasped the prevailing medical idea of lactation as a cause of insanity. She was also exhausted:

> She got a little low and depressed. Things worried her unnecessarily. Husband had no reason to think she was going out of her mind or required care and sup[ervisio] n. Had been exercised in repairing harm done by ceiling falling on carpet and overtaxed her strength 3 days before. About 11 am was washing staircase – child being nursed by the other children and cried. [This contradicts Mary Ann Goldring's testimony at the trial that she was looking after the older children.] Mother went and took it and put it in pail she was using. Then went and told a lodger what she had done.

The note adds that Julia's parents were 'temperate with no insanity' but that her grandfather (her mother's father) was believed to have been in an asylum. This was William Chalkley, who was admitted to Bedford lunatic asylum in June 1858. A note made after admission states that a cousin (her father's brother's son) was also insane. It describes the cause of Julia's insanity as being both 'hereditary' and 'lactation'.

Nicolson seems to have formed a favourable impression of Julia. His notes from 12 February 1889, shortly after she was admitted, describe her as 'a respectable looking woman with a pleasing address and manner'. He records Julia as saying that 'after the birth of her last child she suffered from lowness of spirits, sleeplessness and headaches. She now says she is much improved, sleeps better and feels more cheerful'. He then adds that 'by her manner and appearance she shows a tendency to melancholia'.

In March, however, when Julia was visited by Frederick, he found her 'in bed suffering from headache, suffusion of eyes, crying and very low in spirits. Said one of the patients told her she would have to remain here 5 years'. (In fact, she was to remain in Broadmoor for seven years.)

Throughout the course of 1889 she seems to have become a little happier. By July she is recorded as being 'more cheerful and contented, though she is easily upset when she becomes low spirited and melancholic' and by December she is 'much improved mentally' and 'cheerful and industrious. She sleeps better and her head does not trouble her much'. Her bodily health is 'good'.

The record continues in a similar vein over the next couple of years, with Julia variously described as 'cheerful', 'industrious' and 'rational'. In February 1890, Nicolson's annual report describes Julia as 'rational and tranquil' and says that she 'has steadily improved'. Her bodily health is 'good', her mental condition 'convalescent' and in response to a question as to whether she was harmless he writes: 'She is making satisfactory progress – but it would not be advisable to discharge her until her mental strength is more fully restored. It is only just a year since she was admitted.'

By July 1891, she was in Ward 2 – the intermediate ward – and working in the scullery. It all seemed to be going so well. But everything changed on 9 December 1891, at which point Julia had been in Broadmoor nearly two years:

> For the last few days she has been noticed as looking a little dull and not replying in her usual responsive manner. This evening when another patient [name redacted] went into the scullery with her mug, she said to this patient,

> I have finished my supper. Spickernell gave a short answer and then apparently losing all control caught up the mug and threw it at [name redacted] striking her on the left cheek. Spickernell removed to infirmary.

A day later Julia was described as 'restless during the night. Eyes suffused. Bowels confined. Seems sorry for what she has done. Says that at the time it appeared to her as if [name redacted] was trying to annoy her'.

Two months later, she had 'settled down from the excited condition she was in but is very low spirited and listless'. By October she was back on Ward 2 but had 'not fully got over her last attack. Seems low and down hearted'.

Sadly, Julia's low mood continued. Even in 1893 her manner was described as 'serious and depressed' and 'very different from her former cheerful and active appearance'.

Progress seems to have been slow. Over the next two years there were gradual improvements but she was still, in November 1895, 'reserved and uncommunicative'. By April 1896, she was 'rational, orderly, quiet and cheerful'.

Despite her mental state, Frederick was very keen to have Julia home, and it wasn't long after her admission that he started making representations to the Home Office asking for his wife to be released. The Home Office wrote to Broadmoor four times: in January 1890 ('Mr F. H. Spickernell prays for his wife's release: thinks she is sufficiently recovered to be released with safety'), September 1890, April 1895 and January 1896. To the first request, the response from Broadmoor was that Julia was 'much improved – and now rational and tranquil – But it was a case of murder (she drowned her child 9 months old) only a year ago and Nicolson thinks she should not be released till her mental strength is more fully restored. Decline to discharge in the usual terms.'

Not long after Julia was admitted to Broadmoor, Frederick and the children moved to 21, Jubilee Villas (a recent build, judging by the name) in Wanstead, and Julia's sister Harriet moved in with them to look after the children. The 1891 census records Harriet as 'living on her own means' – though it seems more likely that Frederick was paying for her upkeep. It must have been a hard time for Frederick, who, while Julia was in Broadmoor, lost both his parents in quick succession: his mother in November 1894 and his father in August 1895.

A letter from Broadmoor to the Home Office dated 17 April 1895 refers to Julia's insanity as 'partly hereditary, partly due to lactation'. It describes Julia as 'rational and in good health' and refers to a relapse three years earlier, from which she has now recovered. However, the letter concludes, 'Dr Nicolson thinks it would not be desirable to release her yet.' Another note five days later refers to a 'civil letter to husband expressing regret – but as it is a case of relapse it will not do to hold out hopes at present'.

By the start of 1896, Julia's prospects were clearly improving. Enclosed with a letter from the Home Office, dated 13 January, is a letter from Frederick to the secretary of state, referring to the 'many visits I have made to my Wife extending over a number of years,' in which he has 'found her to be in good health both mentally and physically and to be hopefully looking forward to an early restoration to her Family'. Frederick adds that he hopes the home secretary will conclude that Julia's health is 'permanent' and that she is 'perfectly safe to return to her home'. He has 'taken every precaution for her future safety and happiness by her sister Miss Edwards permanently living with her affording my wife every protection'.

For good measure, Frederick himself wrote directly to Nicolson on the same date, from his new address, 153, Ramsay Road, Forest Gate in east London. The letter makes clear that Frederick had spoken to Nicolson on his last visit, on 26 December, and refers to the 'encouraging account of her progress under your care'. He encloses a copy of his letter to the secretary of state, and says he hopes 'that it will have a successful issue after so many years of patient and anxious waiting her restoration to me and her family'. He repeats his commitment to having Julia's sister live with them.

Nicolson's philosophy was actively to encourage visits from family, though Frederick was probably unusual, amongst Broadmoor relatives, in the frequency with which he visited his wife. His letters seem to show genuine affection for Julia and a desire to have her home, as well as an ease and confidence in his dealings with Nicolson.

A note from Nicolson dated 28 February 1896 reads:

> If Mrs Spickernell goes on as satisfactorily for a further period of 6 months as she has been for the past 2 years I think her case might be favourably considered, especially as her husband occupies a good position in the Post Office Department and is prepared to have his wife's sister always at their home to look after her.

Julia was now 44, but there is no mention of the menopause as a possible reason either to delay her release or to expedite it. Although it was believed that while women were still capable of getting pregnant, there was a risk of puerperal insanity making a reappearance, Jonathan Andrews has noted that 'concern about future child-bearing was rarely a decisive factor on its own in justifying patients' continuing detention'.[29] Both the medical superintendents and the Home Office balked at the idea of detaining women for many years after they had 'to all intents and purposes recovered'.

On the other hand, Andrews writes, 'patients' level of education … and assessments of the educational backgrounds of their family and kin on the same grounds had real bearing on patients' suitability for discharge.'[30] This was certainly the case for Julia, with Frederick's good job (and possibly his fluent letters) counting strongly in her favour.

After seven years in Broadmoor, Julia was discharged on 5 October 1896, and joined her family, now comfortably ensconced in the suburbs. The mid- to late nineteenth century had seen the railways extend to outer London, and from the 1860s on, the advent of the underground system enabled more and more white-collar workers to move out of central London.[31] The railway had arrived at Wanstead in 1856, and at Forest Gate in 1858, so it is likely that Frederick commuted to work.[32] The Spickernells' new homes would have been modern and well equipped.

In 1901, Frederick and Julia were living in Cann Hall, Essex, with son Frederick, 19, and daughter Edith, 15, a 'pupil teacher'. Their elder daughter, Emily, was living at Whitelands Training College in Chelsea, where she was studying to become a teacher – an increasingly popular profession for young women, as the introduction of universal primary education had created more demand for teachers.[33] Despite Frederick's promise to Broadmoor, Harriet had by now left the Spickernells' home and was living with her mother, aunt and cousin in Stevenage.

As was standard, Frederick had to issue three-monthly reports on Julia's mental health. On 11 February 1905, he wrote to the medical superintendent from their new address, 7, Knighton Road, Forest Gate, asking that he be allowed to discontinue the reports because Julia 'has been in first class health ever since she has been home and am satisfied that she will continue to enjoy good health'.

From that time on, the family seems to have flourished – though one puzzle is why they moved so frequently. Was it down to economic factors, or did the notoriety of Julia's crime, Spickernell not being a common name, make them unwelcome in some neighbourhoods? Andrews suggests that families were often so worried about the stigma attached to infanticide that, after release they would move to a place where they were unknown.

By 1911, Frederick and Julia had found their permanent home: 2, Drummond Road, in Wanstead, where they lived with their three adult children. Emily and Edith, now aged 30 and 25, were elementary schoolteachers, while Frederick, 29, was working as a correspondence clerk. To have three adult children at home must have been unusual, and two of them remained single for the rest of their lives. Frederick senior, now 58, was still a telegraphist, and the family remained well-off enough to employ a domestic servant, 19-year-old Eva Mold.

Frederick and Julia stayed in Drummond Road for the rest of their married life. They seem to have had a comfortable retirement. When Frederick died on 16 January 1937 at the age of 84, he left £896 (equivalent to about £64,000 today). In old age, Julia was cared for by her adult children. Two years after her husband's death, she was still at Drummond Road, now 'incapacitated', living with her unmarried son, Frederick, only 57, but retired from his work as a stenographer.

Julia survived another five years, dying in Oster House, a St Albans hospital, in 1944 at the age of 91 and leaving a substantial sum of £1,420. The death was registered by her daughter Emily Baker. Emily, who had married in 1924, now lived in Clarence Road, St Albans, so it seems she had brought her mother to be near her at the end.

The three children appear to have remained close. Emily herself was to die just over a year after Julia, leaving the St Albans house to her siblings: both Edith and Frederick lived at Clarence Road until their deaths in 1960 and 1967 respectively.

It is impossible for us to know whether Julia's life after Broadmoor was a happy one, but she seems to have been luckier than many in similar situations. Her experience illustrates important features of late-Victorian attitudes towards female criminality: the emphasis on the distinctive nature of female biology as a cause of insanity; a belief in the importance of respectability and previous good character as deciding factors in determining whether a defendant was insane; and a willingness to stretch the legal definition of criminal insanity to accommodate cases where the defendant was aware of what she was doing. At Broadmoor, Julia's condition seems to have been treated with sensitivity by Nicolson and his staff, and she was allowed frequent visits from her husband. The prevailing view was clearly that Julia's particular kind of insanity was temporary and curable.

Julia's story is perhaps most notable for the closeness of her immediate family: despite her crime, she seems to have been supported by a loving husband, sister and children. Far from disrupting the family bond, Julia's experience may even have strengthened it.

Bibliography

Archival sources

The Broadmoor Criminal Lunatic Asylum Archive, Berkshire Record Office, Coley Avenue, Reading, Berkshire:

Patient case file of Eliza Blanche Bastable D/H14/D2/2/273

Patient case file of Mary France D/H14/D2/2/2/404

Patient case file of Rebecca Loveridge D/H14/D2/2/2/365

Patient case file of Mary Ann Mellor D/H14/D2/2/2/146

Patient case file of Julia Georgina Spickernell D/H14/D2/2/2/431

Patient case file of Rebecca Turton D/H14/D2/2/2/21

Patient case file of Elizabeth White D/H14/D2/2/2/442

Reports upon Broadmoor Criminal Lunatic Asylum 1864–1895 D/H14/A2/1/1

Admissions Register 1872–1901 D/H14 A1/1/1/2

Disposal Register 1872–1901 D/H14 A1/2/1/2

Other

Dorset County Lunatic Asylums, *The Annual Report of the Dorset County Lunatic Asylums Charminster and Forston for the year 1877* (Dorchester, 1878)

Dorset County Lunatic Asylums, *The Annual Report of the Dorset County Lunatic Asylums Charminster and Forston for the year 1878* (Dorchester, 1879)

Primary sources: books

Anonymous, *The Servants' Practical Guide: A Handbook of Duties and Rules* (Frederick Warne & Co, London, 1880)

Beeton, Isabella, *Mrs Beeton's Book of Household Management* (Ward, Lock & Co, London, 1907)

Booth, Charles, *Life and Labour of the People in London* (Macmillan, London, 1892)

Brabner, J. H. F., *The Comprehensive Gazetteer of England & Wales, 1894–5* (London, 1997)

Children's Employment Commission, *Second Report of the Commissioners: Trades and Manufactures* (HMSO, London, 1843)

Farrer, William & Brownbill, J., *A History of the County of Lancaster: Volume 4* (London, 1911)

Great Britain. Parliament. House of Commons. *Parliamentary Papers, volume 32* (HMSO, London, 1892)

Lewis, Samuel (ed), *A Topographical Dictionary of England* (London, 1848), British History Online at www.british-history.ac.uk/topographical-dict/england [accessed 31 March 2021].

Mayhew, Henry, *Labour and the Poor, vol. 1: The Metropolitan Districts* (Ditto Books, London, 2019)

Smith, Albert et al., *Gavarni in London: Sketches of London Life and Character* (David Bogue, London, 1849)

Primary sources: journals

Baker, John, 'Female Criminal Lunatics: A Sketch', *Journal of Mental Science*, 48:200 (1902), pp. 13–28

Chadwick, David, 'On the Rate of Wages in Manchester and Salford, and the Manufacturing Districts of Lancashire, 1839–59', *Journal of the Statistical Society of London*, 23:1 (1860), pp. 1–36

Gilbert, William, 'A visit to a convict lunatic asylum', *Cornhill Magazine* (1864), p. 449

Nicolson, David, 'The Measure of Individual and Social Responsibility in Criminal Cases', *The Journal of Mental Science*, 24:105 (1878), pp. 1–25 & pp. 249–73

Tuke, John, 'Cases Illustrative of the Insanity of Pregnancy, Puerperal Mania, and Insanity of Lactation', *Edinburgh Medical Journal*, 12:2 (1867), pp. 1083–1101

Wynter, Andrew, *Our Social Bees; or, Pictures of Town & Country Life, and other papers* (Forgotten Books, London, 2018)

Primary sources: online

Accessed through Ancestry.com

Board of Guardian Records and Church of England Parish Registers, London Metropolitan Archives, London

Commissioners in Lunacy, 1845–1913, Lunacy Patients Admission Registers, The National Archives, Kew, England

Electoral Registers, London, England: London Metropolitan Archives

England, Births and Christenings, 1538–1975, Salt Lake City, Utah

England, Wales and Scotland Census 1841, Kew, Surrey, England: The National Archives of the UK

England Censuses 1851–1911, Kew, Surrey, England: The National Archives of the UK

England, Cheshire Bishop's Transcripts, 1576–1933, Salt Lake City, Utah

England, Marriages, 1538–1973, Salt Lake City, Utah

General Register Office, England and Wales Civil Registration Indexes

Lancashire Anglican Parish Register, Preston, England: Lancashire Archives

Principal Probate Registry, Calendar of the Grants of Probate and Letters of Administration made in the Probate Registries of the High Court of Justice in England

Wigan Anglican Parish Registers, Wigan Archives Services, Wigan, England

Other primary sources

British History Online at www.british-history.ac.uk

Hitchcock T, R., Shoemaker, C. Emsley, S. Howard & J. McLaughlin, et al., *The Old Bailey Proceedings Online, 1674–1913*, at www.oldbaileyonline.org

Office for National Statistics, Homicide in England and Wales: year ending March 2019 at www.ons.gov.uk/peoplepopulationandcommunity/crimeandjustice/articles/homicideinenglandandwales/yearendingmarch2019

The British Newspaper Archive at www.britishnewspaperarchive.co.uk

The Imperial Gazetteer of England and Wales, 1872, vol. 2 at https://tinyurl.com/y45w8vxl

Secondary sources

Appignanesi, Lisa, *Mad, Bad and Sad: A History of Women and the Mind Doctors from 1800 to the Present* (Virago, London, 2011)

Arnold, Catharine, *Bedlam: London and its Mad* (Simon & Schuster, London, 2008)

Atsushi Fukao, Junta Takamatsu, Takeshi Arishima, Mika Tanaka, Toshio Kawai, Yasuki Okamoto, Akira Miyauchi, Akihisa Imagawa, 'Graves' disease and mental disorders', *Journal of Clinical & Translational Endocrinology*, 19 (March 2020,100207)

Barnsby, George, 'The Standard of Living in the Black Country during the Nineteenth Century', *The Economic History Review*, 24(2) (1971), pp. 220–39

Barnsby, George, *A History of Housing in Wolverhampton 1750–1975* (Integrated Publishing Services, Wolverhampton, 1986)

Benson, J, *British Coalminers in the Nineteenth Century: A Social History* (Longman Higher Education, London, 1989)

Bourke, Joanna, *Working-class Cultures in Britain 1890–1960: Gender, Class and Ethnicity* (Routledge, London, 1996)

Bourke, Joanna 'Childbirth in the UK: suffering and citizenship before the 1950s', *The Lancet*, 383: 9924 (2014), pp. 1288–9

Broderick, Eugene (2005), 'Religion and class in nineteenth-century Ireland: The social composition of Waterford's Anglican community, 1831–71'. *Saothar, 30*, pp. 61–71.

Burnett, John (ed), *Useful Toil: Autobiographies of Working People from the 1820s to the 1920s* (Allen Lane, London, 1974)

Busfield, Joan, 'The Female Malady? Men, Women and Madness in Nineteenth Century Britain', *Sociology*, 28:1 (1994), pp. 259–77

Challinor, Raymond, *The Lancashire and Cheshire Miners* (Graham, Newcastle upon Tyne, 1972)

Chamberlain, Geoffrey, 'British maternal mortality in the 19th and early 20th centuries', *Journal of the Royal Society of Medicine*, (November 2006) 99 (11): pp. 559–63

Chapman, Stanley (ed), *The History of Working-class Housing, A Symposium* (David & Charles, Newton Abbott, 1971)

Crossick, Geoffrey (ed), *The Lower Middle Class in Britain 1870 to 1914* (Routledge, London, 2016)

Davies, Caitlin, *Bad Girls: A History of Rebels and Renegades* (John Murray, London, 2018)

Dodenhoff, Jenna '"A dangerous kind": Domestic violence and the Victorian middle class', *TCNJ Journal of Student Scholarship*, vol. X (April 2008)

Donnelly, James, *The Land and the People of Nineteenth-Century Cork* (Routledge, Abingdon, 2018)

Drife, James 'The start of life: a history of obstetrics', *Postgraduate Medical Journal* 78 (2002), pp. 311–15

Dyhouse, Carol, 'Working-Class Mothers and Infant Mortality In England, 1895–1914' *Journal of Social History,* 12:2 (1978), pp. 248–67

Engels, Friedrich, *The Condition of the Working Class in England* (George Allen & Unwin, London, 1943)

Flanders, Judith, *The Victorian House: Domestic Life from Childbirth to Deathbed* (HarperPerennial, London, 2004)

Forsythe, Bill & Melling, Joseph (eds), *Insanity, Institutions and Society, 1800–1914* (Routledge, London, 1999)

French, Christopher, 'Taking up "the challenge of micro-history": social conditions in Kingston upon Thames in the late nineteenth and early twentieth centuries', *The Local Historian*, 36:1 (2006), pp. 17–28

Godfrey, Barry, Richardson, Jane & Walklate, Sandra, 'Domestic Abuse in England and Wales 1770–2020'. Working Paper No. 2. Domestic Abuse: Responding to the Shadow Pandemic. University of Liverpool. (2020)

Goose, Nigel, 'Poverty, old age and gender in nineteenth-century England: the case of Hertfordshire', *Continuity and Change*, 20:3 (2005), pp. 351–84

Gordon, Harvey, *Broadmoor: An Inside Story* (Psychology News Press, London, 2012)

Griffiths, Trevor, *The Lancashire Working Classes c.1880–1930* (OUP, Oxford, 2001)

Hardy, Thomas, *Tess of the d'Urbervilles* (Macmillan & Co, London, 1912)

Hardy, Thomas, *Jude the Obscure* (Bantam Classics, New York, 2008)

Hardy, Thomas & Hardy, Florence, *The Life of Thomas Hardy 1840–1928* (London, Wordsworth Editions, 2007)

Headrick, Daniel R. & Griset, Pascal, 'Submarine telegraph cables: Business and politics, 1838–1939' *Business History Review*, 75:3 (Autumn 2001), pp. 543–78

Historic England, *19th- and 20th-Century Roman Catholic Churches* (Historic England, London, 2017)

Horn, Pamela, 'The Dorset Dairy System'. *The Agricultural History Review* 26:2 (1978), pp. 100–7

Hoskins, William, *The Making of the English Landscape* (Book Club Associates, London, 1981)

Jackson, John T., 'Nineteenth Century Housing in Wigan and St. Helens', *Transactions of the Historic Society of Lancashire and Cheshire,* 129 (1980), pp. 125–43

Jackson, Lee (ed), *Daily Life in Victorian London: An Extraordinary Anthology* (Victorian London Ebooks, 2011)

Jackson, Mark, *Infanticide: Historical Perspectives on Child Murder and Concealment, 1550–2000* (Routledge, London, 2002)

John, Angela, *By the Sweat of their Brow: Women Workers at Victorian Coal Mines* (Routledge, London, 1984)

Jump, Harriet Devine (ed), *Women's Writing of the Victorian Period 1837–1901: An Anthology* (Edinburgh University Press, Edinburgh, 1999)

Kohn, George C., *Encyclopedia of Plague and Pestilence: From Ancient Times to the Present* (Facts on File, New York, 2008)

Knight, Charles, *Knight's Cyclopaedia of London, 1851* (Charles Knight, London, 1851)

Lacey, Nicola, 'Psychologising Jekyll, Demonising Hyde: The Strange Case of Criminal Responsibility', *LSE Law, Society and Economy Working Papers*, London School of Economics and Political Science (2009)

Liddington, Jill & Norris, Jill, *One Hand Tied Behind Us* (Rivers Oram Press, London, 2000)

Lockwood, David, *The Blackcoated Worker* (George Allen & Unwin, London, 1958)

Long, Jason, 'The surprising social mobility of Victorian Britain', *European Review of Economic History*, 17:1 (February 2013), pp. 1–23

McLeod, Hugh, *Religion and Society in England, 1850–1914* (Basingstoke, 1996)

Magnússon, Sigurður Gylfi & Szijártó, István, *What is Microhistory?* (Taylor & Francis, London, 2013)

Marland, Hilary, *Dangerous Motherhood: Insanity and Childbirth in Victorian Britain* (Palgrave, London, 2004)

Moran, James, Topp, Leslie & Andrews, Jonathan (eds), *Madness, Architecture and the Built Environment: Psychiatric Spaces in Historical Context* (Routledge, London, 2007)

Moran, Richard, 'The origin of insanity as a special verdict: the trial for treason of James Hadfield', *Law and Society Review,* 19:3 (1980), pp. 487–519

Pooley, Sian, 'Parenthood, child-rearing and fertility in England, 1850–1914', *The History of the Family* (2013) 18(1): pp. 83–106.

Porter, Roy, *A Social History of Madness: Stories of the Insane* (Phoenix Giants, London, 1987)

Reay, Barry, *Microhistories: Demography, Society and Culture in Rural England, 1800–1930* (CUP, Cambridge, 2002)

Rubenhold, Halle, *The Five: The Untold Lives of the Women Killed by Jack the Ripper* (Doubleday, London 2019)

Sauer, R, 'Infanticide and abortion in nineteenth-century Britain', *Population Studies*, 32:1 (1979), pp. 81–93

Scull, Andrew, *Museums of Madness: the Social Organization of Insanity in Nineteenth-Century England* (Penguin, Harmondsworth, 1979)

Shaw-Taylor, Leigh, 'Family farms and capitalist farms in mid nineteenth century England'. *The Agricultural History Review*. 53: 2(2005), pp. 158–91

Shepherd, Jade, '"One of the Best Fathers until He Went Out of His Mind": Paternal Child-Murder, 1864–1900', *Journal of Victorian Culture*, 18:1 (2013), pp. 1–19

Shepherd, Jade, 'Female Friendships and Family Roles at Broadmoor', blogpost (1 June 2014) at https://voicesfrombroadmoor.wordpress.com/2014/06/01/female-friendships-and-family-roles

Shepherd, Jade, '"I am very glad and cheered when I hear the flute": The Treatment of Criminal Lunatics in Late Victorian Broadmoor', *Medical History*, 60:4 (2016), pp. 473–91

Shepherd, Jade, 'Life for the families of the Victorian Criminally Insane', *The Historical Journal,* 63:3 (2020), pp. 603–32

Showalter, Elaine, *The Female Malady: Women, Madness and English Culture, 1830–1980* (Virago, London, 1993)

Sloan, Barry, 'An Anxious Discourse: English Rural Life and Labour and the Periodical Press between the 1860s and the 1880s' (2013) pre-print, University of Southampton Institutional Repository

Stevens, Mark, *Broadmoor Revealed: Victorian Crime and the Lunatic Asylum* (Pen & Sword, Barnsley, 2013)

Sullivan, Nikki & Hawkins, Cathy, 'Broadmoor's Early "Pleasure Women", or the Somatics of Maternal Filicide in Late Nineteenth-Century Britain', *Somatechnics*, 9:2–3 (2019)

Taylor, David, *The New Police in Nineteenth-Century England* (Manchester University Press, Manchester, 1997)

Thompson, Edward, *The Making of the English Working Class* (Pelican, Middlesex, 1982)

Thompson, Francis M. L., 'Nineteenth-Century Horse Sense', *The Economic History Review*, 29:1 (1976), pp. 60–81

Thompson, Francis M. L., *The Rise of Suburbia* (Palgrave Macmillan, London, 1982)

Thompson, Francis M. L., *The Cambridge Social History of Britain 1750–1950: Volume 2, People and their Environment* (CUP, Cambridge, 1990)

Todd, Selina, *Snakes and Ladders* (Chatto & Windus, London, 2021)

Trinder, Barrie, *The Making of the Industrial Landscape* (JM Dent & Sons, London, 1982)

Ward, Tony, 'The sad subject of infanticide: law, medicine and child murder, 1860–1938', *Social & Legal Studies*, 8:2 (1999), pp. 163–80

Webster, Richard, *Why Freud was Wrong* (HarperCollins, London, 1996)

Zedner, Lucia, *Women, Crime, and Custody in Victorian England* (Clarendon Press, Oxford, 1991)

Theses and dissertations

Bailey, Amie, *Sex and Madness: Exploring Male and Female Experiences in Broadmoor and Bethlem Hospitals,* BA dissertation, University of Reading (2018)

Heller, Michael, *London Clerical Workers 1880–1914: The Search for Stability*, PhD thesis, University College London (2003)

MacKenzie, Charlotte, *A Family Asylum: A History of the Private Madhouse in Ticehurst, Sussex, 1792–1917*, PhD thesis, University of London (1986)

Pedley, Alison, '*A painful case of a woman in a temporary fit of insanity': A study of women admitted to Broadmoor Criminal Lunatic Asylum between 1863 and 1884 for the murder of their children*, MA thesis, University of Roehampton (2012)

Pedley, Alison, *'A deed at which humanity shudders': Mad mothers, the law and the asylum, c. 1835–1895,* PhD thesis, University of Roehampton (2020)

Stilwell, Martin, *Victorian Heroes: Peabody, Waterloo and Hartnell: the Development of Housing for the Working-Classes in Victorian Southwark*, Master's dissertation in local history, Kingston University (2015)

Stokeld, Rosalind Joan Grace, *The impact on Borough Market of the arrival of railways up to 1885* (2019), MA thesis, University of York (2019)

Wilcox, Laura, *Exploring Female Madness through the Moulsford Lunatic Asylum Records*, MA thesis, University of Reading (2013)

Websites

GB Historical GIS / University of Portsmouth, Kingsteignton AP/CP through time | Population Statistics | Males and Females, *A Vision of Britain through Time* at www.visionofbritain.org.uk/unit/10132836/cube/GENDER

History of Chatterton Village at https://thehistoryofchattertonvillage.wordpress.com

Keegan, Vic, 'Vic Keegan's Lost London 52: the Devil's Acre' (blogpost published 3 August 2018) at www.onlondon.co.uk/vic-keegans-lost-london-52-the-devils-acre/

St Andrew Holborn at www.standrewholborn.org.uk/www.holbornvenues.co.uk

Wilkinson, Amanda, Victorian Occupations at http://victorianoccupations.co.uk

Wolverhampton History & Heritage at www.historywebsite.co.uk/articles/VictorianBuildings/19thCentWolves.htm

Notes

Chapter 1: The Road to Broadmoor

1. H. Gordon, *Broadmoor* (Psychology News Press, London, 2012), p. 22
2. A. T. Scull, *Museums of Madness: the Social Organization of Insanity in Nineteenth-Century England* (Penguin, Harmondsworth, 1979), p. 13
3. ibid., p. 14
4. C. Arnold, *Bedlam: London and its Mad* (Simon & Schuster, London, 2008), p. 24
5. ibid., p. 24
6. ibid., p. 43
7. A. T. Scull, *Museums of Madness: The Social Organization of Insanity in Nineteenth-Century England* (Penguin, Harmondsworth, 1979), p. 24
8. ibid., p. 75
9. ibid., p. 23
10. C. MacKenzie, *A Family Asylum: A History of the Private Madhouse in Ticehurst, Sussex, 1792–1917* (PhD thesis, University of London, 1986) p. 37
11. A. T. Scull, *Museums of Madness: The Social Organization of Insanity in Nineteenth-Century England* (Penguin, Harmondsworth, 1979), p. 25
12. ibid., p. 34
13. ibid., p. 36
14. ibid., p. 41

15. E. Showalter, *The Female Malady: Women, Madness and English Culture, 1830–1980* (Virago, London, 1993), p. 31
16. Quoted in A. T. Scull, *Museums of Madness: the Social Organization of Insanity in Nineteenth-Century England* (Penguin, Harmondsworth, 1979), p. 109
17. A. T. Scull, *Museums of Madness: The Social Organization of Insanity in Nineteenth-Century England* (Penguin, Harmondsworth, 1979), p. 113
18. E. Showalter, *The Female Malady: Women, Madness and English Culture, 1830–1980* (Virago, London, 1993), p. 23
19. ibid., p. 24
20. A. T. Scull, *Museums of Madness: The Social Organization of Insanity in Nineteenth-Century England* (Penguin, Harmondsworth, 1979), p. 195
21. ibid., p. 244
22. ibid., p. 252
23. ibid., p. 170
24. E. Showalter, *The Female Malady: Women, Madness and English Culture, 1830–1980* (Virago, London, 1993), p. 8
25. A. T. Scull, *Museums of Madness: The Social Organization of Insanity in Nineteenth-Century England* (Penguin, Harmondsworth, 1979), p. 14
26. C. MacKenzie, *A Family Asylum: A History of the Private Madhouse in Ticehurst, Sussex, 1792–1917* (PhD thesis, University of London, 1986), p. 142
27. H. Monro, quoted in A. T. Scull, *Museums of Madness: The Social Organization of Insanity in Nineteenth-Century England* (Harmondsworth, 1979), p. 235
28. R. Webster, *Why Freud was Wrong* (HarperCollins, London, 1996) p. 85.
29. E. Showalter, *The Female Malady: Women, Madness and English Culture, 1830–1980* (Virago, London, 1993), p. 204
30. ibid., p. 52

31. J. Busfield, 'The Female Malady? Men, Women and Madness in Nineteenth Century Britain', *Sociology*, 28 (1) (1994), p. 268
32. E. Showalter, *The Female Malady: Women, Madness and English Culture, 1830–1980* (Virago, London, 1993), p. 55
33. R. Webster, *Why Freud was Wrong* (Harper Collins, London, 1996) p. 57
34. Quoted in E. Showalter, *The Female Malady: Women, Madness and English Culture, 1830–1980* (Virago, London, 1993), p. 56
35. S. Pooley, 'Parenthood, child-rearing and fertility in England, 1850–1914'. *Hist Fam.* 18(1), (2013) pp. 83–106
36. J. Bourke, 'Childbirth in the UK: suffering and citizenship before the 1950s', *The Lancet*, 383: 9924, (April 2014), pp. 1288–9
37. G. Chamberlain, 'British maternal mortality in the 19th and early 20th centuries', *Journal of the Royal Society of Medicine*, (November 2006): 99 (11): pp. 559–63
38. C. Dyhouse, 'Working-Class Mothers and Infant Mortality in England, 1895–1914', *Journal of Social History*, 12(2) (1978), pp. 248–67
39. J. Bourke, *Working-Class Cultures in Britain 1890–1960: Gender, Class and Ethnicity* (Routledge, London, 1996), p. 7
40. J. Drife, 'The start of life: a history of obstetrics', *Postgraduate Medical Journal*, 78 (2002), p. 313
41. R. Porter, *A Social History of Madness: Stories of the Insane* (Phoenix Giants, London, 1987), p. 103
42. H. Marland, '"Destined to a perfect recovery": The confinement of puerperal insanity in the nineteenth century', in J. Melling & B. Forsythe (eds), *Insanity, Institutions and Society, 1800–1914* (Routledge, London, 1999), p. 153
43. ibid., p. 154
44. D. Nicolson, 'The Measure of Individual and Social Responsibility in Criminal Cases', *The Journal of Mental Science*, 24: 106 (1878), p. 264

45. H. Marland, 'Getting away with murder? Puerperal insanity, infanticide and the defence plea' in M. Jackson, *Infanticide: Historical Perspectives on Child Murder and Concealment, 1550–2000* (London, 2002), p. 177
46. L. Appignanesi, *Mad, Bad and Sad: A History of Women and the Mind Doctors from 1800 to the Present* (Virago, London, 2011), p. 89
47. H. Marland, '"Destined to a perfect recovery": The confinement of puerperal insanity in the nineteenth century', in B. Forsythe & J. Melling (eds), *Insanity, Institutions and Society, 1800–1914* (Routledge, London, 1999), p. 166
48. ibid, p. 164
49. J. Tuke, 'Cases Illustrative of the Insanity of Pregnancy, Puerperal Mania, and Insanity of Lactation', *Edinburgh Medical Journal*, 12 (2) (1867), p. 1097
50. H. Marland, '"Destined to a perfect recovery": The confinement of puerperal insanity in the nineteenth century', in B. Forsythe & J. Melling (eds), *Insanity, Institutions and Society, 1800–1914* (Routledge, London, 1999), p. 158
51. E. Showalter, *The Female Malady: Women, Madness and English Culture, 1830–1980* (Virago, London, 1993), p. 54
52. L. Wilcox, *Exploring Female Madness through the Moulsford Lunatic Asylum Records*, MA thesis, University of Reading (2013), pp. 16–20
53. R. Moran, 'The origin of insanity as a special verdict: the trial for treason of James Hadfield', *Law and Society Review* Vol 19, issue 3 (1980), p. 499
54. M. Stevens, *Broadmoor Revealed: Victorian Crime and the Lunatic Asylum* (Pen & Sword, Barnsley, 2013), p. 5
55. A. Pedley, '*A painful case of a woman in a temporary fit of insanity': A study of women admitted to Broadmoor Criminal Lunatic Asylum between 1863 and 1884 for the murder of their children*, MA thesis, University of Roehampton (2012), p. 18

56. D. Nicolson, 'The Measure of Individual and Social Responsibility in Criminal Cases', *The Journal of Mental Science*, vol. 24, no. 105 (1878)
57. L. Zedner, *Women, Crime, and Custody in Victorian England* (OUP, Oxford, 1991), p. 34
58. ibid, p. 38
59. Office for National Statistics, Homicide in England and Wales: year ending March 2019 at www.ons.gov.uk/peoplepopulationandcommunity/crimeandjustice/articles/homicideinenglandandwales/yearendingmarch2019
60. H. Gordon, *Broadmoor* (Psychology News Press, London, 2012), p. 128
61. L. Zedner, *Women, Crime, and Custody in Victorian England* (Oxford, 1991), p. 38
62. R. Sauer, 'Infanticide and abortion in nineteenth-century Britain', *Population Studies*, vol. 32, no. 1 (1979), p. 85
63. ibid., p. 81
64. H. Marland 'Getting away with murder? Puerperal insanity, infanticide and the defence plea', in M. Jackson, *Infanticide: Historical Perspectives on Child Murder and Concealment, 1550–2000* (Routledge, London, 2002), p. 170
65. See e.g. M. Arnot, 'The murder of Thomas Sandles: meanings of a mid-nineteenth-century infanticide' in M. Jackson (ed.), *Infanticide: Historical Perspectives on Child Murder and Concealment* (Routledge, London, 2002), pp.149–67
66. H. Marland 'Getting away with murder? Puerperal insanity, infanticide and the defence plea', in M. Jackson, *Infanticide: Historical Perspectives on Child Murder and Concealment, 1550–2000* (Routledge, London, 2002),p. 170
67. R. Sauer, 'Infanticide and abortion in nineteenth-century Britain', *Population Studies*, vol. 32, no. 1 (1979), p. 82
68. L. Zedner, *Women, Crime, and Custody in Victorian England* (Oxford, 1991), p. 39

69. N. Sullivan & C. Hawkins, 'Broadmoor's Early "Pleasure Women", or the Somatics of Maternal Filicide in Late Nineteenth-Century Britain', *Somatechnics*, 9: 2–3 (2019)
70. H. Gordon, *Broadmoor* (Psychology News Press, London, 2012), p. 126
71. N. Sullivan & C. Hawkins, 'Broadmoor's Early "Pleasure Women", or the Somatics of Maternal Filicide in Late Nineteenth-Century Britain', *Somatechnics*, 9: 2–3 (2019)
72. H. Marland, 'Getting away with murder? Puerperal insanity, infanticide and the defence plea', in M. Jackson, *Infanticide: Historical Perspectives on Child Murder and Concealment, 1550–2000* (Routledge, London, 2002), p. 175
73. ibid., p. 172
74. ibid., p. 183
75. ibid. p. 176
76. T. Ward, 'The sad subject of infanticide: law, medicine and child murder, 1860–1938', *Social & Legal Studies*, 8:2 (1999), p. 167
77. H. Marland, *Dangerous Motherhood: Insanity and Childbirth in Victorian Britain* (Palgrave, London, 2004), p. 181
78. H. Marland 'Getting away with murder? Puerperal insanity, infanticide and the defence plea' in M. Jackson, *Infanticide: Historical Perspectives on Child Murder and Concealment, 1550–2000* (Routledge, London, 2002), p. 179
79. ibid., p. 179
80. ibid., p. 181
81. J. Baker, 'Female Criminal Lunatics: a Sketch', *Journal of Mental Science*, 48:200 (1902), p. 15
82. T. Ward, 'The sad subject of infanticide: law, medicine and child murder, 1860–1938', *Social & Legal Studies*, 8:2 (1999), p. 166
83. H. Marland, 'Getting away with murder? Puerperal insanity, infanticide and the defence plea' in M. Jackson, *Infanticide:*

Historical Perspectives on Child Murder and Concealment, 1550–2000 (Routledge, London, 2002), p. 171

84. M. Arnot, 'The Murder of Thomas Sandles', in M. Jackson, *Infanticide: Historical Perspectives on Child Murder and Concealment, 1550–2000* (Routledge, London, 2002), p. 160
85. L. Zedner, *Women, Crime, and Custody in Victorian England* (OUP, Oxford, 1991), p. 89
86. H. Marland 'Getting away with murder? Puerperal insanity, infanticide and the defence plea', in M. Jackson, *Infanticide: Historical Perspectives on Child Murder and Concealment, 1550–2000* (Routledge, London, 2002), p. 172
87. J. Shepherd, '"One of the Best Fathers until He Went Out of His Mind": Paternal Child-Murder, 1864–1900', *Journal of Victorian Culture*, 18:1 (2013), p. 12
88. H. Gordon, *Broadmoor* (Psychology News Press, London, 2012), p. 13
89. D. Weiner, '"This coy and secluded dwelling": Broadmoor Asylum for the criminally insane' in J. Moran, L. Topp & J. Andrews (eds) (2007), *Madness, Architecture and the Built Environment: Psychiatric Spaces in Historical Context* (London, Routledge), p. 138
90. M. Stevens, *Broadmoor Revealed: Victorian Crime and the Lunatic Asylum* (Pen & Sword, Barnsley, 2013), p.13
91. D. Weiner, '"This coy and secluded dwelling": Broadmoor Asylum for the criminally insane' in J. Moran, L. Topp & J. Andrews (eds) (2007) *Madness, Architecture and the Built Environment: Psychiatric Spaces in Historical Context* (London, Routledge), p. 140
92. A. Pedley, '*A painful case of a woman in a temporary fit of insanity': A study of women admitted to Broadmoor Criminal Lunatic Asylum between 1863 and 1884 for the murder of their children*, MA thesis, University of Reading (2012), p. 49

93. H. Gordon, *Broadmoor* (Psychology News Press, London, 2012), p. 17
94. Broadmoor Criminal Lunatic Asylum, *Reports of the superintendent and chaplain of Broadmoor Criminal Lunatic Asylum 1864* (London, 1865), p. 10
95. ibid., p. 7
96. ibid., p. 8
97. ibid., p. 10
98. H. Gordon, *Broadmoor* (Psychology News Press, London, 2012), p. 22
99. M. Stevens, *Broadmoor Revealed: Victorian Crime and the Lunatic Asylum* (Pen & Sword, Barnsley, 2013), p.7
100. Broadmoor Criminal Lunatic Asylum; R. Southey, P. Palmer, C. Phillips, T. Ashe, D. Nicolson, Reports upon *Broadmoor Criminal Lunatic Asylum, with statistical tables, for the year 1887* (London, 1888), p. 6
101. M. Stevens, *Broadmoor Revealed: Victorian Crime and the Lunatic Asylum* (Pen & Sword, Barnsley, 2013), p.9
102. Quoted in A. Bailey, *Sex and Madness: exploring male and female experiences in Broadmoor and Bethlem Hospitals* (BA dissertation, University of Reading) (2018)
103. See e.g. A. T. Scull, *Museums of Madness: The Social Organisation of Insanity in Nineteenth-Century England* (Penguin, Harmondsworth, 1979), p. 170
104. M. Stevens, *Broadmoor Revealed: Victorian Crime and the Lunatic Asylum* (Pen & Sword, Barnsley, 2013), p. 2
105. J. Andrews, 'The boundaries of Her Majesty's Pleasure: discharging child-murderers from Broadmoor and Perth Criminal Lunatic Department, c. 1860 to 1920' in M. Jackson, *Infanticide: Historical Perspectives on Child Murder and Concealment, 1550–2000* (Routledge, London, 2002), p. 235
106. M. Stevens, *Broadmoor Revealed: Victorian Crime and the Lunatic Asylum* (Pen & Sword, Barnsley, 2013), p. 15

107. ibid., p. 15
108. Broadmoor Criminal Lunatic Asylum; R. Southey, P. Palmer, C. Phillips, T. Ashe, D. Nicolson, *Reports upon Broadmoor Criminal Lunatic Asylum, with statistical tables, for the year 1887* (London, 1888), p. 47
109. M. Stevens, *Broadmoor Revealed: Victorian Crime and the Lunatic Asylum* (Pen & Sword, Barnsley, 2013), p. 15
110. Broadmoor Criminal Lunatic Asylum; R. Southey, P. Palmer, C. Phillips, T. Ashe, D. Nicolson, *Reports upon Broadmoor Criminal Lunatic Asylum, with statistical tables, for the year 1887* (London, 1888),
111. ibid., p. 78
112. M. Stevens, *Broadmoor Revealed: Victorian Crime and the Lunatic Asylum* (Pen & Sword, Barnsley, 2013), p. 3
113. ibid., p.
114. Broadmoor Criminal Lunatic Asylum, *Reports upon Broadmoor Criminal Lunatic Asylum, with statistical tables, for the year 1864* (London, 1865)
115. J. Shepherd, 'Female Friendships and Family Roles at Broadmoor', blogpost 1 June 2014 at https://voicesfrombroadmoor.wordpress.com/2014/06/01/female-friendships-and-family-roles
116. J. Shepherd, 'Life for the families of the Victorian Criminally Insane.' *The Historical Journal* 63(3), pp. 603–32
117. ibid.
118. ibid.
119. ibid.
120. M. Stevens, *Broadmoor Revealed: Victorian Crime and the Lunatic Asylum* (Pen & Sword, Barnsley, 2013), p. 15
121. ibid., p. 24
122. See e.g. the description of life at Colney Hatch asylum in A. Scull, *Museums of Madness: The Social Organisation of Insanity in Nineteenth-Century England* (Penguin, Harmondsworth, 1979), p. 196

123. J Shepherd, '"I am very glad and cheered when I hear the flute": The Treatment of Criminal Lunatics in Late Victorian Broadmoor', *Medical History*, 60:4 (2016), p. 484
124. ibid., p. 484
125. Winchester, quoted in H. Gordon, *Broadmoor* (Psychology News Press, London 2012), p. 31
126. J. Andrews, 'The boundaries of Her Majesty's Pleasure: discharging child-murderers from Broadmoor and Perth Criminal Lunatic Department, c. 1860 to 1920' in M. Jackson, *Infanticide: Historical Perspectives on Child Murder and Concealment, 1550–2000* (Routledge, London, 2002), p. 218
127. ibid., p. 224
128. ibid., p. 225
129. ibid., p. 233
130. ibid., p. 246
131. C. French, 'Taking up 'the challenge of micro-history': social conditions in Kingston upon Thames in the late nineteenth and early twentieth centuries', *The Local Historian*, 36:1 (2006), p. 17
132. H. Rubenhold, *The Five: The Untold Lives of the Women Killed by Jack the Ripper* (London, Doubleday, 2019)

Chapter 2: Mary France

1. S. Lewis, *A Topographical Dictionary of England*, seventh edition (London, 1848), p. 100
2. A. John, *By the Sweat of their Brow: Women Workers at Victorian Coal Mines* (London, 1984), p. 107
3. R. Challinor, *The Lancashire and Cheshire Miners* (Graham, Newcastle upon Tyne, 1972), p. 67
4. D. Chadwick, 'On the Rate of Wages in Manchester and Salford, and the Manufacturing Districts of Lancashire, 1839–59', *Journal of the Statistical Society of London*, 23:1 (March 1860), p. 18

5. F. Engels, *The Condition of the Working Class in England* (London, 1943), p. 258
6. J. Benson, *British Coalminers in the Nineteenth Century: A Social History* (Longman Higher Education, London, 1989), p. 65
7. ibid., p. 254
8. F. Engels, *The Condition of the Working Class in England* (George Allen & Unwin, London, 1943), p. 248
9. J. T. Jackson, 'Nineteenth Century Housing in Wigan and St. Helens', *Transactions of the Historic Society of Lancashire and Cheshire,* 129 (January 1980), p. 125
10. J. Benson, *British Coalminers in the Nineteenth Century: A Social History* (Longman Higher Education, London, 1989), p. 119
11. Quoted in R. Challinor, *The Lancashire and Cheshire Miners* (Graham, Newcastle upon Tyne, 1972), p. 243
12. E. P. Thompson, *The Making of the English Working Class* (Pelican, Middlesex, 1982), p. 361
13. R. Challinor *The Lancashire and Cheshire Miners* (Graham, Newcastle upon Tyne, 1972), p. 245
14. ibid., p. 246
15. ibid., p. 247
16. ibid., p. 248
17. A. John, *By the Sweat of their Brow: Women Workers at Victorian Coal Mines* (Routledge, London, 1984), p. 121
18. H. McLeod, *Religion and Society in England 1850 to 1914* (Macmillan, Basingstoke, 1996), p. 65
19. ibid., p. 28
20. ibid., p. 84
21. ibid., p. 98
22. ibid., p. 25
23. J. Liddington & J. Norris, *One Hand Tied behind Us* (Rivers Oram Press, London, 2000) p. 79

24. ibid., p. 89
25. D. Chadwick, 'On the Rate of Wages in Manchester and Salford, and the Manufacturing Districts of Lancashire, 1839–59', *Journal of the Statistical Society of London*, 23:1 (March 1860), p. 5
26. F. Engels, *The Condition of the Working Class in England* (George Allen & Unwin, London, 1943), p. 164
27. A. John, *By the Sweat of their Brow: Women Workers at Victorian Coal Mines* (Routledge, London, 1984), p. 121
28. ibid., p. 188
29. M. Anderson, 'The social implications of demographic change', in F. M. L. Thompson (ed), *The Cambridge Social History of Britain, 1750–1950, Volume 2: People and their Environment* (CUP, Cambridge, 1990), p. 35
30. A. John, *By the Sweat of their Brow: Women Workers at Victorian Coal Mines* (Routledge, London, 1984), p. 118
31. B. Reay, *Microhistories: Demography, Society and Culture in Rural England, 1800–1930* (CUP, Cambridge, 2002), p. 113
32. J. Benson, *British Coalminers in the Nineteenth Century: A Social History* (Longman Higher Education, London, 1989), pp. 122–3
33. M. Anderson, 'The social implications of demographic change', in FML Thompson (ed), *The Cambridge Social History of Britain, 1750–1950, Volume 2: People and their Environment* (CUP, Cambridge, 1990), p. 64
34. A. John, *By the Sweat of their Brow: Women Workers at Victorian Coal Mines* (Routledge, London, 1984), p. 97
35. J. Benson, *British Coalminers in the Nineteenth Century: A Social History* (Longman Higher Education, London, 1989), p. 106
36. J. Bourke, *Working-Class Cultures in Britain 1890–1960: Gender, Class and Ethnicity* (Routledge, London, 1996), p. 7
37. J. Benson, *British Coalminers in the Nineteenth Century: A Social History* (Longman Higher Education, London, 1989), p. 6

38. 'Local and district news', *Bolton Evening News*, (5 September 1881), p. 2
39. J. Benson, *British Coalminers in the Nineteenth Century: A Social History* (Longman Higher Education, London, 1989), p. 129
40. F. Atsushi et al., 'Graves' disease and mental disorders' *Journal of Clinical & Translational Endocrinology*, 19 (2020)
41. 'The child murder at Aspull: Extraordinary delusions', *Manchester Evening News* (22 December 1886), p. 4
42. 'Murder near Bolton', *Manchester Courier and Lancashire General Advertiser* (20 December 1886), p. 8
43. 'The child murder at Aspull: Extraordinary delusions', *Manchester Evening News* (22 December 1886), p. 4
44. A. Pedley, '*A deed at which humanity shudders': Mad mothers, the law and the asylum, c.1835–1895*, PhD thesis, University of Roehampton (2020)
45. T. Griffiths, *The Lancashire Working Classes c.1880–1930* (OUP, Oxford, 2001), p. 221
46. 'Shocking child murder at Aspull', *Cumberland & Westmoreland Herald* (25 December 1886), p. 6
47. 'The child murder at Aspull: Extraordinary delusions', *Manchester Evening News* (22 December 1886), p. 4
48. 'The Aspull Murder Case', *Wigan Observer and District Advertiser* (29 January 1887), p. 5
49. ibid, p. 5
50. *Reports upon Broadmoor Criminal Lunatic Asylum, with statistical tables, for the year 1887* (London, 1888), p. 2
51. ibid., p. 22
52. ibid., p. 4
53. ibid., p. 9
54. ibid., p. 6
55. ibid. p. 9
56. J. Andrews, 'The boundaries of Her Majesty's Pleasure: discharging child-murderers from Broadmoor and Perth

Criminal Lunatic Department, c. 1860 to 1920' in M. Jackson, *Infanticide: Historical Perspectives on Child Murder and Concealment, 1550–2000* (Routledge, London, 2002), p. 224

57. J. Andrews, 'The boundaries of Her Majesty's Pleasure: discharging child-murderers from Broadmoor and Perth Criminal Lunatic Department, c. 1860 to 1920' in M. Jackson, *Infanticide: Historical Perspectives on Child Murder and Concealment, 1550–2000* (Routledge, London, 2002), p. 231
58. 'Consecration of Daisy Hill Church', *Bolton Evening News* (22 April 1881), p. 3
59. J. Andrews, 'The boundaries of Her Majesty's Pleasure: discharging child-murderers from Broadmoor and Perth Criminal Lunatic Department, c. 1860 to 1920' in M. Jackson, *Infanticide: Historical Perspectives on Child Murder and Concealment, 1550–2000* (Routledge, London, 2002), p. 231
60. ibid., p. 231
61. R. Challinor, *The Lancashire and Cheshire Miners* (Graham, Newcastle upon Tyne, 1972), p. 191

Chapter 3: Mary Ann Meller

1. M. Stilwell, *Victorian Heroes: Peabody, Waterloo and Hartnell: the Development of Housing for the Working-Classes in Victorian Southwark*, Master's dissertation in local history, Kingston University (2015)
2. H. Mayhew, *Labour and the Poor, vol. 1: The Metropolitan Districts* (London, Ditto books, 2019), p. 2
3. R. J. G. Stokeld, The impact on Borough Market of the arrival of railways up to 1885 (2019), MA thesis, University of York
4. ibid.

5. M Stilwell, *Victorian Heroes: Peabody, Waterloo and Hartnell: the Development of Housing for the Working-Classes in Victorian Southwark*, Master's dissertation in local history, Kingston University (2015)
6. ibid.
7. C. Knight, *Knight's Cyclopaedia of London, 1851* (Charles Knight, London, 1851)
8. J. Flanders, *The Victorian House: Domestic Life from Childbirth to Deathbed.* (HarperPerennial, London, 2004)
9. T. Miller, 'Carmen and coal heavers' in A. Smith et al., *Gavarni in London: Sketches of London Life and Character* (David Bogue, London, 1849), p. 65
10. H. Broadhurst, 'Stonemason', from John Burnett (ed), *Useful Toil: Autobiographies of Working People from the 1820s to the 1920s* (Allen Lane, London, 1974), p. 313
11. ibid. p. 319
12. C. Booth, *Life and Labour of the People in London* (Macmillan, London, 1892)
13. 'Southwark', report in *Morning Advertiser*, Monday, 4 November 1867, p. 7
14. 'Attempt to murder a woman', *Lloyd's Weekly Newspaper*, Sunday, 3 November 1867, p. 3
15. Letter from Charles Dickens to *The Times*, 13 November 1849.
16. 'Discoveries at Horsemonger-Lane Gaol', *Reynold's Newspaper*, Sunday 12 August 1888, p. 6
17. Broadmoor Criminal Lunatic Asylum: *Reports of the superintendent and chaplain of Broadmoor Criminal Lunatic Asylum, for the year 1868,* p. 5
18. ibid., p. 12
19. Edward Walford, 'The Old Kent Road', in Old and New London: vol. 6 (London, 1878), pp. 248–55. British History Online at www.british-history.ac.uk/old-new-london/vol6/pp248–255 [accessed 22 March 2021]

Chapter 4: Elizabeth White

1. Historic England, *19th- and 20th-Century Roman Catholic Churches* (Historic England, London, 2017), p. 7
2. W. Hoskins, *The Making of the English Landscape* (Book Club Associates, London, 1981), p. 224
3. G. Barnsby, *A History of Housing in Wolverhampton 1750–1975* (Integrated Publishing Services, Wolverhampton, 1986)
4. Quoted in B. Trinder, *The Making of the Industrial Landscape* (J. M. Dent & Sons, London, 1982), p. 187
5. G. Barnsby, 'The Standard of Living in the Black Country during the Nineteenth Century.' *The Economic History Review*, 24(2) (1971), pp. 220–39
6. G. Barnsby, *A History of Housing in Wolverhampton 17501975* (Integrated Publishing Services, Wolverhampton, 1986), p. 10
7. Children's Employment Commission, *Second Report of the Commissioners: Trades and Manufactures* (HMSO, London, 1843), p. 33
8. 'Wolverhampton Protestant Alliance', *Wolverhampton Chronicle and Staffordshire Advertiser* (4 February 1852, p. 2)
9. Wolverhampton History & Heritage website at www.historywebsite.co.uk/articles/VictorianBuildings/19thCentWolves.htm
10. I. Beeton, *Mrs Beeton's Book of Household Management* (Ward, Lock & Co, 1907), p. 1767
11. Anonymous, *The Servants' Practical Guide: A Handbook of Duties and Rules* (Frederick Warne & Co., London, 1880), p. 165
12. Information about Bethnal Green Asylum from *Parliamentary Papers, volume 32* (HMSO, London, 1892)
13. *Old Bailey Proceedings Online* (www.oldbaileyonline.org, version 8.0, 30 March 2021), January 1890, trial of ELIZABETH WHITE (38) (t18900113-129).

14. C. Davies, *Bad Girls: A History of Rebels and Renegades* (John Murray, London, 2018)
15. Broadmoor Criminal Lunatic Asylum, *Reports upon Broadmoor Criminal Lunatic Asylum, with statistical tables, for the year 1891* (HMSO, London, 1892)
16. Obituary of George Dunn from *The Times* (11 March 1912), p. 11
17. 'Shocking accident on the Wycombe Branch Railway', *South Bucks Standard* (9 May 1902), p. 2

Chapter 5: Blanche Bastable

1. T. Hardy, *Jude the Obscure* (Bantam Classics, New York, 2008) p. 242
2. L. Shaw-Taylor, 'Family farms and capitalist farms in mid nineteenth century England'. *The Agricultural History Review*. 53; 2(2005), pp. 158–91
3. P. Horn, 'The Dorset Dairy System'. *The Agricultural History Review* 26:2 (1978), pp. 100–7
4. ibid., p. 100
5. T. Hardy, *Tess of the d'Urbervilles* (Macmillan & Co, London, 1912), pp. 449–50
6. Cited in B. Sloan, 'An Anxious Discourse: English Rural Life and Labour and the Periodical Press between the 1860s and the 1880s'. (2013) pre-print, University of Southampton Institutional Repository
7. The club-men were groups of local vigilantes who tried to protect their local areas against the behaviour of the two sides in the English civil war, stopping their property being damaged, for example, or their wives and daughters from being raped.
8. T. Hardy and F. Hardy, *The Life of Thomas Hardy 1840–1928* (London, Wordsworth Editions, 2007)
9. 'Shroton', *Western Gazette*, Friday 29 September 1876, p. 8

10. 'A mother killed by her daughter', *Salisbury and Winchester Journal* (10 November 1877), p. 6
11. *The Annual Report of the Dorset County Lunatic Asylums Charminster and Forston for the year 1877* (Dorchester, 1878), p. 9
12. *The Annual Report of the Dorset County Lunatic Asylums Charminster and Forston for the year 1878* (Dorchester, 1879), p. 13
13. *Broadmoor Criminal Lunatic Asylum: Reports upon Broadmoor Criminal Lunatic Asylum, with statistical tables, for the year 1878*
14. *Broadmoor Criminal Lunatic Asylum: Reports upon Broadmoor Criminal Lunatic Asylum, with statistical tables, for the year 1880*
15. ibid.
16. J. Shepherd (2020), 'Life for the families of the Victorian criminally insane'. *The Historical Journal, 63*(3), pp. 603–32.
17. 'Shot himself in Fit of Temper: Tragic Death of East Orchard Boy', *Western Gazette* (Friday, 3 December 1848), p. 2

Chapter 6: Rebecca Loveridge

1. V. Keegan, 'Vic Keegan's Lost London 52: the Devil's Acre' (blogpost published 3 August 2018) at www.onlondon.co.uk/vic-keegans-lost-london-52-the-devils-acre
2. H. Mayhew, *London Labour and the London Poor* (Wordsworth Editions Ltd, Ware, 2008), p. 9
3. A. Wilkinson, 'H is for Hawker' (blogpost published 9 January 2015) at http://victorianoccupations.co.uk/h/h-is-for-hawker
4. 'Petty sessions', newspaper report in *Cardiff Times* (5 July 1861), p. 7
5. GB Historical GIS / University of Portsmouth, Kingsteignton AP/CP through time | Population Statistics | Males and

Females, *A Vision of Britain through Time* at www.visionofbritain.org.uk/unit/10132836/cube/GENDER [accessed 30 March 2021]

6. F. M. L. Thompson, 'Nineteenth-Century Horse Sense', *The Economic History Review*, 29:1 (1976), pp. 60–81
7. F. P. Cobbe, 'Wife Torture in England', in H. D. Jump (ed) *Women's Writing of the Victorian Period 1837–1901: An Anthology* (Edinburgh University Press, Edinburgh, 1999), p. 223
8. B. Godfrey, J. Richardson and S. Walklate, 'Domestic Abuse in England and Wales 1770–2020. Working Paper No. 2. Domestic Abuse: Responding to the Shadow Pandemic' (University of Liverpool. July 2020)
9. J. Dodenhoff, '"A dangerous kind": Domestic violence and the Victorian middle class', *TCNJ Journal of Student Scholarship*, vol. 10, (April 2008)
10. 'Prisoner committed for trial', *East and South Devon Advertiser* (19 January 1884), p. 4
11. ibid.
12. 'Discharged prisoners' aid society', *Exeter and Plymouth Gazette Daily Telegrams* (30 January 1884), p. 3
13. Broadmoor Criminal Lunatic Asylum, *Reports upon Broadmoor Criminal Lunatic Asylum, with statistical tables, for the year 1885* (Eyre & Spottiswoode, London,1887)
14. 'Breach of warranty at Totnes', *Chard and Ilminster News* (29 July 1893), p. 2

Chapter 7: Rebecca Turton

1. E. Broderick (2005). 'Religion and class in nineteenth-century Ireland: The social composition of Waterford's Anglican community, 1831–71'. *Saothar, 30*, 61–71. Retrieved February 8, 2021, from www.jstor.org/stable/23199799

2. J. Donnelly (2018), *The Land and the People of Nineteenth-Century Cork* (Abingdon, Routledge), p. 19
3. A. Wilkinson, 'D is for dressmaker', from Amanda Wilkinson's Victorian Occupations blog (12 December 2013) at http://victorianoccupations.co.uk/d/d-is-for-dressmaker
4. G. F. Pardon, 'The Popular Guide to London and its Suburbs' (1862) from *Daily Life in Victorian London: An Extraordinary Anthology,* ed. Lee Jackson (2011), Victorian London Ebooks
5. 'Bromley Common in the early 1800s': blogpost at https://thehistoryofchattertonvillage.wordpress.com/bromley-common-in-the-early-1800s
6. 'Alleged murder of a husband by his wife' *Belfast Mercury* (26 April 1854), p. 3
7. ibid.
8. J. Greenwood (1874), 'The Wilds of London', from *Daily Life in Victorian London: An Extraordinary Anthology*, ed. Lee Jackson (2011), Victorian London Ebooks
9. W. Gilbert, 'A visit to a convict lunatic asylum', *Cornhill Magazine* (1864), p. 449
10. ibid. p. 453
11. ibid. p. 459
12. 'Murder of a female lunatic', *Salisbury and Winchester Journal* (26 June 1858), p. 7
13. J. Donnelly, *The Land and the People of Nineteenth-Century Cork* (Routledge, Abingdon, 2018), p. 235

Chapter 8: Julia Spickernell

1. *The Imperial Gazetteer of England and Wales, 1872*, vol. 1, p. 75 at https://tinyurl.com/y5denoqs
2. GB Historical GIS/University of Portsmouth, East Hertfordshire District through time, Industry Statistics

Standard Industrial Classification (2007), by sex at www.visionofbritain.org.uk/unit/10211979/cube/INDUSTRY_GEN_SEX [accessed 23 September 2019]

3. N. Goose, 'Poverty, old age and gender in nineteenth-century England: the case of Hertfordshire', *Continuity and Change*, 20:3 (2005)
4. D. Taylor, *The New Police in Nineteenth-century England: Crime, Conflict and Control* (Manchester, 1997), p. 70
5. G. C. Kohn, *Encyclopedia of Plague and Pestilence: From Ancient Times to the Present* (Facts on File, New York, 2008), p. 52
6. St Andrew Holborn at www.standrewholborn.org.uk/www.holbornvenues.co.uk
7. I. Beeton, *Mrs Beeton's Book of Household Management*, publisher (Ward, Lock & Co, London, 1907), p. 1172
8. A. S. Wohl, 'The Housing of the Working Classes in London 1815–1914), in S. Chapman (ed), *The History of Working-class Housing, A Symposium* (David & Charles, Newton Abbott, 1971), p. 15
9. A. P. Baggs, Diane K. Bolton and Patricia E. C. Croot, 'Islington: Growth', in T. F. T. Baker & C. R. Elrington (eds), *A History of the County of Middlesex: Volume 8, Islington and Stoke Newington Parishes*, eds. (London, 1985), pp. 9–19. British History Online at www.british-history.ac.uk/vch/middx/vol8/pp9-19
10. M. Heller, *London Clerical Workers 1880–1914: The Search for Stability* (2003, unpublished PhD thesis, University College London), p. 5
11. H. McLeod, 'White collar values and the role of religion', in G. Crossick (ed), *The Lower Middle Class in Britain 1870–1914* (Routledge, London, 2016), p. 84
12. J. Long, 'The surprising social mobility of Victorian Britain', *European Review of Economic History*, 17:1 (February 2013), p. 10

13. S. Todd, *Snakes and Ladders* (Allen Lane, London, 2021), p. 50
14. G. L. Anderson, 'The social economy of late-Victorian clerks', in G. Crossick (ed), *The Lower Middle Class in Britain 1870–1914* (Routledge, London, 2016), p. 114
15. D. Lockwood, *The Blackcoated Worker* (George Allen & Unwin, London, 1958), p. 28
16. A. Wynter, *Our Social Bees; or, Pictures of Town & Country Life, and other papers* (Forgotten Books, London, 2018), p. 289
17. G. Crossick, 'The emergence of the lower middle class in Britain: a discussion', in G. Crossick (ed.), *The Lower Middle Class in Britain 1870 to 1914* (Routledge, London, 2016), p. 27
18. J. Flanders, *The Victorian House: Domestic Life from Childbirth to Deathbed* (London, HarperPerennial, 2004)
19. Mentioned in the report of the inquest, *London Evening Standard* (2 January 2 1889), p. 2
20. D. R. Headrick & P. Griset, 'Submarine telegraph cables: Business and politics, 1838–1939', *Business History Review*, 75:3 (Autumn 2001), p. 546
21. Report of the inquest, *London Evening Standard* (2 January 1889), p. 2
22. Old Bailey Proceedings Online (www.oldbaileyonline.org, version 8.0, 24 September 2019), February 1889, trial of JULIA GEORGINA SPICKERNELL (37) (t18890204-214).
23. 'Police Intelligence', *London Evening Standard* (7 January 1889), p. 2
24. 'The child murder at Stoke Newington: Inquest and Verdict' *Islington Gazette* (3 January 1889), p. 3
25. N. Lacey, 'Psychologising Jekyll, Demonising Hyde: The Strange Case of Criminal Responsibility', *LSE Law, Society and Economy Working Papers*, London School of Economics and Political Science (2009)

26. D. Nicolson, 'The Measure of Individual and Social Responsibility in Criminal Cases', *The Journal of Mental Science*, 24:105 (1878), p. 11
27. *Reports upon Broadmoor Criminal Lunatic Asylum, with statistical tables, for the year 1889* (London, 1890), p. 5
28. ibid., p. 11
29. J. Andrews, 'The boundaries of Her Majesty's Pleasure: discharging child-murderers from Broadmoor and Perth Criminal Lunatic Department, c. 1860 to 1920' in M. Jackson, *Infanticide: Historical Perspectives on Child Murder and Concealment, 1550–2000* (London, 2002), p. 231
30. ibid., p. 236
31. F. M. L. Thompson, *The Rise of Suburbia* (Palgrave Macmillan, London, 1982), p. 19
32. W. R. Powell (ed), *A History of the County of Essex: Volume 6* (London, 1973) 43–50. British History Online at www.british-history.ac.uk/vch/essex/vol6/pp43-50
33. S. Todd, *Snakes and Ladders* (Chatto & Windus, London, 2021), p. 29